A Baker's Dozen
The Way It Was

Canada

*The Publishers acknowledge the financial assistance of the
Government of Canada through the Book Publishing Industry Development Program
(BPIDP) for our publishing activities.*

Library and Archives Canada Cataloguing in Publication

Murray, Pearl, 1927-
    A baker's dozen : the way it was / Pearl Murray.

ISBN 978-0-88887-397-2

    1. Bidulock family. 2. Frontier and pioneer life–Alberta–
Hairy Hill Region. 3. Hairy Hill Region (Alta.)–Biography.
I. Title.

FC3695.H34Z48 2010   971.23'3   C2010-903156-3

A Baker's Dozen
The Way It Was

Pearl Murray

Borealis Press
Ottawa, Canada
2010

Maria

She crossed the Atlantic
At the age of five
Times were hard
Would they survive

That winter they huddled
In a house topped with sod
Had food from the land
And faith in God

When she was ten
Her mother died
Her father was left
Five children to guide

With sisters and brothers
She helped all she could
To cook and to wash
And to gather the wood

When a young lady
She ran into Fred
It was instant love
And soon they were wed

On an Alberta homestead
Near a picturesque pond
A baker's dozen
Soon ran all around

She taught them well
To work and to care
When the war came along
She had much more to bear

Her sons joined the Air Force
Tranquillity lost
Then her first-born sailed
The sea she once crossed

Her children married
They came by with their crew
A batch of little ones
The family tree grew

She counted her blessings
Thanked God every day
For health and for guidance
Along life's way

I loved Maria
She was like no other
For you see
Maria was my mother

Contents

Preface: The Way It Was

I began recording childhood memories of my life on a homestead about a baker's dozen years ago, but that is not the reason for the book's title.

Although I had no real plans for a book, over time, as stories accumulated, it became evident that something had to be done. With much difficulty and the use of magnifiers (I am legally blind), I researched the possibility of publishing. But I was not getting anywhere fast. Then one day, two fine ladies offered to help. The offer was one I could not refuse. However, during our early discussions I remembered that a huge celebration was being planned for the farm: its 100th anniversary. Our hope was to do the book in time for the occasion. We had only seven or eight months at our disposal. So it was by the grace of God, and the hard work of my helpers, that the book took shape.

My parents, Fred and Maria Bidulock, had thirteen children—a baker's dozen. From oldest to youngest they were John, Gladys, Mike, Daniel, Helen, Nick, Steve, Kathleen (Katie), Pearl, George, Lucille, Bertha (Beth), and Adeline. Sadly, in 1937, that number was reduced to an even dozen when brother Mike (age nineteen) died. While helping a neighbour with cutting wood, he became extremely chilled. Illness followed and he did not respond to Mother's constant care. Medical exams and X-rays determined he had tuberculosis and could benefit at a sanitarium in Calgary. There, an attempt to remove an infected lung was not successful.

Fall Rainbow over the farm taken from the front door of the house. 2007.
Photo: Adeline Peake

The Rainbow

A colourful arch
Embraces the land
One arm in the river
One touches the pond

The arch is a sign
Of goodness and hope
The pasture is green
Wheat sways its head

The hayloft bulges
The garden grows
The udders are full
Eggs wait in the nest

Soft raindrops fall
Create a new bow
Of hues so soft
Red, yellow and blue

There's hope in a rainbow
That embraces all
From lake to river
From river to pond

Photographs

The photographs are from a family collection that was almost lost. In the mid-1990s, several years after my parents were deceased, I visited the farm. While there I looked through Mother's albums and was appalled to discover that many pages were blank; photos had been removed! That initiated a request to the family to get the photos back. The response was not quite, but almost 100 per cent. The originals were then taken to a printer and copies made available to the families. To make that possible, my husband David Murray did the footwork, organized the photographs, and typed the captions; a time-consuming and stressful undertaking—they were to be ready for a family reunion.

All reunions have been held at the homestead where a grandson and his wife, Reg (Steve's son) and Brenda Bidulock, reside and make constant improvements.

The "Rainbow" photograph was taken from the site where the summer-house stood. Credit goes to Adeline Peake, a sister and avid photographer.

Paintings

The paintings and sketches are by the author. Following is a write-up shared in my latest show in October 2009, at the Strathcona Senior Centre. My conviction is that writing and painting go "hand in hand." They are both dependent on experiences and observations. I would also like to acknowledge Bill Lorenz as the artist who painted the picture of the granary.

About the Artist

During her early years on an Alberta homestead, Pearl Murray was surrounded by nature—trees, flowers, and lakes. It is no wonder that her interest in art lies mostly in landscape. During those early years, not knowing what art was all about, she sketched and coloured in secret. But later art became her major at the University of Alberta.

Although she began in oils, she was eager to explore other media—watercolour, pastels, silk screening, papermaking, batik, black ink, etching, pottery, brass rubbings (in England), and other art forms that crossed her path.

As a member of the Federation of Canadian Artists and later the Society of Western Canadian Artists, Pearl rubbed shoulders with many who shared her interest. Over the years she enjoyed guidance from dedicated artists including Harry Savage, Jerry Heine, and Francis Alte-Arscott, and participated in workshops in Jasper with Gregg Johnson. The workshops were held in the fall when nature's colours were at their best.

Pearl continued to paint in spite of macular degeneration that robbed her of most of her vision. A fellow painter referred to her as "Edmonton's Monet" because her style had become quite impressionistic.

Acknowledgements

Primarily, I wish to thank a kindly and enthusiastic editing team, Lily McCool and Ardith Trudzik (author of *Freckles, The Core of My Apple,* and *If You Tell*) who, aware of my visual disability, and my commitment as caregiver to my husband Dave who struggles with Lewy Body disease, had offered to help me. I regard that as a godsend. As well, I wish to thank our children, Donald Murray, Douglas Murray, Natalie Stevens, and Charlene Ritchie, who encouraged, edited, and helped with photographs and computer problems; thanks to Jack Bilsland and the Creative Writing Group at Strathcona Senior Centre, especially Jim Graham and Kay Dier, for encouraging and helpful remarks; to Alec Maier, who early in my writing endeavours advised, "If you are stuck, write about what you know"; to Margot Neis who, after reading only my first few stories, suggested that they would be of interest to schools and internationally. I wish to thank Writers in Residence at the University of Alberta for suggestions over the years. And I am most grateful to my husband Dave, who provided me with a computer and taught me the basic skills, including how to type in 48 point font and then reduce it to normal print. I am also grateful to the CNIB for a CCTV (closed circuit television)—a "mega" magnifier.

*To my parents Fred and Maria Bidulock, whose
courage and dedication to family and land was beyond
expectation. Through guidance and example they taught love
and kindness, honesty, humility, and commitment.*

Introduction

In the old days of the Canadian west, there was a farm. It started before I was born, sometime back before the Great War. It wasn't much of a farm really, just some lines drawn on a map in northern Alberta. It was the middle of nowhere, up past Hairy Hill a ways, on a dead-end gravel road that hit the south bank of the North Saskatchewan River. There were a couple quarters squished in the river's bend to the north, but they faced away from the sun in winter and so were dark places, though in summer they had the best blueberry patches for miles. Our farm held a low ridge on its north boundary that sloped gently away south. That was where the house stood, facing southward across the lake, though it was really just a twenty-acre slough. The land on the hill was sandy, but that's why it was a good place to build—because the soil there could produce no crop. When the skies were clear, the windows of that mud and timber homestead were filled with sunlight, and it brought warmth even on cold days. There was good fresh water from an excellent well, and a long view of the road due south. You could see anybody approaching from a mile away. In other parts of the farm centuries of wind had cast down layers of earth to which scrub brush and poplar now clung; and there were meadows of long grass too. But the thing that made the quarter unique was in the northwest corner the river nipped her edge, and in the deep shade of that steep valley's north face, a rich sloping thicket of firs and evergreens grew.

It doesn't sound like much, I know, but it was from there that we grew a great tree, a tree of life, with many branches, flowers, and fruits. For it was from there that we came, literally born on that soil, my twelve brothers and sisters. All that we have, indeed all I shall ever have, I owe to that simple farm. Yet someone had to tend her, to release her hidden promise—a careful combination of dreamers and stewards. That's what made our big family special, for each had his talents, his strength or his wit, his stamina or his courage; and together we forged a team not only of survival, but of experience and wonder. For land was no guarantee. Indeed we were bordered by those for whom it failed, for whom it brought forth only misery and sorrow. But our father had a keen eye, and steel in his spine, and the sparkle of an old gypsy. For it was Father who had chosen among the vortex of lines, and I see now how well he cast our die. He had no money, no machinery, no seed, but for a price and a promise he had land. Land, earth, air, trees—it mattered not that by his time only cold creeping quarters to the north were left. It was not the rolling-rich prairies of the south. But it was land, and so it was everything. And so that is where we came from.

The beauty of the farm shaped us; in the pattern of a frosted window, in the buzz of a curious fly. Our essence was etched by those rugged acres, by flower and tree, by rock and by stream. The sky above was our heavenly canvas, upon which daily a majestic panorama was brushed. Clouds of ivory towered above, sheets and skiffs and turrets of rain, squalls and rainbows and sunsets of gold. At night the moon, stars, and lights of the north danced before us, an ethereal sable dusted with jewels. It was a beautiful place, but the struggle was constant. In every element we worked, in mud and sleet and snow, but a warm hand guided us, and we received the natural bounty of the land. Nature runs its course, and though life abounds with a scattered brilliance, things also come to an end. Some days dawn red. It was never easy. Looking back, I confess it was rather hard. But we did not know at that time. And so these are some of the stories . . .

—Remembrances of Pearl Murray
  (by Douglas Murray)

The way it was. 1974.

Chapter 1 The Land

The white house took second place after the barn was built. Aerial photo of homestead taken about 1950.

Centre – garden replaced the sheepfold
Lower right – dark woods
Lower left – lake extends for one half mile
Centre right – summerhouse near spruce
Rear – sawmill prepared logs for the building of the barn
Centre – left of garden – tornado removed roof from small barn
White house and gable – built of logs and clay whitewashed with lime

A young man's dream had almost come true, but not quite. My dad, Fred (*Todor*), not yet the legal age of twenty-one, had filed for and was granted a homestead. But the dream carried a price—a price that demanded brain and brawn. Government-mandated improvements were required within a three-year time limit before the land could legally be his. The daunting task loomed before him as he surveyed his land; woods, lake, and brush surrounded him. The launch was slow. A woman to stand beside him would help.

Dad's eye was drawn to a young Romanian lady who lived in the Shepenitz district some fifteen miles southeast of his farm. She was petite and gentle, a contrast to his feisty demeanour. In spite of her father's disapproval, the two continued to connect. Through letters delivered by friends, she corresponded with the tall and active man she adored. Each letter bore a hand-painted rose in one corner. Soon they married, with only a handful of friends present, and Mom (Maria) was delighted with the few towels she received as a wedding gift.

What did Dad and Mother see around them when they settled on the land? What influenced Dad to choose that particular homestead? What driving force urged them to put their hearts and souls into improving their lot?

Our homestead was in what would become the Deep Lake district, about one hundred miles northeast of Edmonton.

Down the slope in front of their home was a lake (really a slough) that joined a much larger lake in the distance—a lake that covered the area where the neighbouring farms intersected with Dad's land. The rest of the land, except for a large meadow near the south boundary, and a smaller meadow surrounded by willows west of the barnyard, was covered with trees—poplar, birch, spruce, and a tangle of smaller bushes.

Directly ahead, between the lake and our south neighbour, the area was heavily wooded. I specifically remember that because Mother and I carried chopped grain and water to a sow that had her piglets in those woods. The large animal lay behind a fallen tree that was partly held up by its branches, thus creating a simple fence between the animal and us. Mother leaned over the fallen tree and deposited the food in front of the hungry animal.

According to the rules and regulations for homesteaders, certain improvements to the land were required within the first three years. If these were met then the land remained the homesteader's property.

The first few acres of land that Dad broke were the level area in the middle of the farm. At that time Dad owned a team of oxen. The animals were strong

Mother Maria, 1956.

Dad Fred, 1956.

but oh, so very slow. While Dad handled a walking plough, Mother walked alongside with a whip to urge the slow beasts forward. They would just as soon have stopped as taken another step. It was a happy day when sometime later Dad traded the oxen for a team of horses.

However, when the wooded area where we fed the sow was broken, Dad had help from a man who owned a steam engine. I remember it as a big ugly machine with a large tank for water. It did the work well—pulled out roots with ease.

In order to prevent soil erosion, as well as to preserve native vegetation, Dad left swaths of vegetation between fields. Those areas protected choke-cherries, saskatoons, wild rose bushes, wild raspberries and strawberries, and a variety of native flowers. While we were gathering hay or stooking, the berries gave us extra energy to carry on.

It was in a meadow that Dad and Mother had a close encounter with bears. The hay had been cut with a scythe and allowed to dry. One day they gathered the hay with forks and stacked it into haycocks. Later, it would be hauled to the barn to feed the few cows and oxen over the winter. John, their firstborn, was about seven months old. They brought with them a child's wagon that Dad had built and set John in it while they worked. At the end of the day they left the wagon in the meadow and carried the child home. The next day when they returned they saw bears.

Bears were often seen during those early days. But this particular day a cub sat in the wagon and the mother bear had the wagon pole in her paws ready to give the little one a ride!

The western side of the homestead was broken when I was about eleven. Since it was not heavily wooded, Dad did it with horses and the whole family pitched in at root- and rock-picking times. Helen, then nineteen years of age, stayed at home to wash the dishes and prepare soup for lunch. She was very dependable but because she too wanted to work with the gang, we took turns cooking. The first time I had a turn the lunch was a disaster! But Mother miraculously saved the day.

The vegetation left between fields provided a picturesque landscape as well as protection from the elements. After the harvest the cattle were put on the fields to glean grain that was missed during the harvest. During inclement or hot weather, they sought the protection of the trees left by Dad.

Chapter 2 A Baker's Dozen

Mom was almost twenty when her first child, John (*Ewon*), was born. It was a difficult birth. With no mother to help and share her new experience, it must have been a frightening time.

During the early 1900s, new mothers were expected to stay in bed for a whole week after a birth. During the twenty-some years that followed, my mother delivered the baker's dozen, thirteen of us in all. I'm sure the week of required bed rest after each birth was her only respite from an otherwise heavy schedule of caring for an ever-growing family.

All births were registered at the local country post office. Father provided English names. Our Romanian names were not registered. Unfortunately, English was not the postmaster's first language and at least five family members' registered names were misspelled. These errors only surfaced once they reached adulthood and needed accurate identification.

The year after John was born, Gladys (*Sanfira*) joined the family. She was named after Mother's mother. Gladys was followed by Mike (*Mihai*), then Dan (*Metro*). Mom's fifth child, a girl, was named Helen (*Elena*), after Mother's only and dearly loved sister.

That first group of five was close-knit. They walked to school together and helped each other with schoolwork. They played and worked well. My parents depended on them for help with chores and seasonal commitments that came along. Oh yes, there was grumbling and complaining, but every one was expected to help.

The second and middle group in the baker's dozen included Nick (*Nicolai*), Steve (*Stefan*), Kathleen/Katie (*Katrina*), and Pearl (*Pakitsa*). We communicated well with the older group, especially Steve, who was always there willing to help. But we also were close to the younger group when it came along. That group began with George (pronounced *Gee-orgee*, g as in go), followed by three sisters, Lucille (*Domnica*), Bertha/Beth (*Veronca*), and Adeline (*Anitsa*).

George, in the middle of five sisters, was constantly on guard lest he be overruled by the females.

The Romanian names and language were generally used during our family's early years. However, as time went by, we children attended school and English was spoken more and more. During the casual transition, language became a mixed bag; it did not matter what language we used; it was understood. By the time the last group of four came along, our parents spoke a lot of English. Consequently the younger members of the family understood the mother tongue, but found it awkward and humorous to use.

Chapter 3 The Big White House

All of Mother and Dad's children at some time lived in the "big white house" and the summerhouse that was situated north of it, but there were other houses before those were built.

I have a vague recollection of my father mentioning a shack, his first home on the homestead. The shack was quite near the lake—I would think about the middle of the present garden area, which is on the south-facing slope between the big white house and the lake. He lived in it while still a bachelor. I remember a strange story he told us of coming home from cutting hay with a scythe. In his absence an intruder had been in his humble home. As he retrieved his few kitchen utensils from a shelf to prepare a meal, he noticed the stub of a burnt candle and a spent match in the bottom of a cup. He took the cup to the lake a few hundred feet away and quickly washed it out. Even though he was too tired and hungry to dwell on the likely act of witchcraft, he remembered the incident all his life.

It is likely that Dad built his second house in anticipation of his marriage to Mom. The couple had three little ones, John, Gladys, and Mike, when that house met with disaster.

It happened when Dad travelled to Vernon, B.C., to visit his sister Dora Kazamerchuk. He found the Alberta winters severe and while visiting his sister, he scouted the area for the possibility of relocating there for the warmer climate.

Mother and the little ones were left behind. While baking bread, Mother got the stove hot. It is likely that the soot in the chimney caught fire and burned the house. The family escaped but a pig in a lean-to shed attached to the house did not. They also lost the few documents that they possessed.

Dad built another home on the highest point farther north. Even though he could see most of his land from that vantage point, the house bore the brunt of the cold north wind. It was small. Each of the two rooms was about 12 feet square.

With the family growing in numbers, they needed a larger home. So Dad built the white house that we grew up in. The summerhouse served as a temporary residence after the fire while the big house was being built. When the larger house was complete, the little house on the high ground was sold to a farmer near Hairy Hill. Since there was no way of moving the building, the logs were numbered, and the house was dismantled and then put together again in its new location.

By today's standards, the big white house was not big. The main floor was a living/kitchen/dining room. The trap door behind the pantry wall led to the dirt cellar that kept potatoes fresh all winter. Jars of preserves and the occasional wooden boxful of apples (often sent by Mother's sister and brother-in-law, Helen and Mike Cucheran, from Vernon) were also kept in the cool cellar.

The upstairs, one large open room with a double bed in each corner, was full most nights. Later a wall installed in the middle made two rooms. The chimney ran up near the stairs and provided warmth in the winter. A dormer facing south was Dad's attempt at design and light.

All the buildings to that point were built with available materials—logs off the farm. Few nails were used. Logs were shaped at their ends to make them fit and were often reinforced using an old-fashioned drill that made holes for handmade dowels.

Even though most of the buildings, including the summerhouse, had the ends of the logs protruding in the corners, Dad trimmed the ends on the white house. It was special. As well, the logs on that building were squared to make for flat sides. That, I presume, was done by hand, using a hatchet, axe, and hand-saw. What a lot of work! But Dad wished to build a fine house.

The site for the building was excellent except for one thing. On that location the house was protected from north winds by the higher ground behind it. The front view consisted of two lakes joined by a channel and surrounded by willows, poplars, and reeds. The landscape and waterfowl on the lake provided moments of pleasure and a feeling of peace. Upon rising in the morning, one always glanced at the lake and had the feeling that all was well with the world. However, the site presented the problem of stability. With cement for piles unavailable in those times, Dad's challenge was to build a stable building on shifting sand. And he did it using rocks!

Dad discovered a seam of clay east of the granary. Water and straw added to the clay, and mixed by the children stomping it with their bare feet, resulted

Pearl and Dave prepare for wedding east of the big white house, 1956..

in filler for cracks between logs. In the case of the white house, after the filler dried, both the interior and exterior walls were made smooth with coats of soft, pure clay. The final step was a couple of coats of whitewash.

In amazement, from a safe distance, we watched our mother make the whitewash. Lime in powdered form was bought. When added to a bucket of cold water, the mixture bubbled and boiled as it was stirred with a wooden paddle. Often bluing, used in laundry to make white clothes whiter, was added to produce a whiter paint. As well, when fine washed sand was added, the paint adhered to the clay.

Each spring Mother checked the walls. Cracks or holes where the clay had fallen out were refilled and repainted.

In mid-winter one year, our home was almost lost. On our return from school we found the family in shock. That day Lucille, who was about five

The big house comes down! 1973.

years old, was bored. She had gone upstairs, found a candle, lit it, and proceeded to make wax dots on the trunk near a curtained window. She had seen older siblings make dots of wax on their hands and called them measles. But she got too near the curtains. When they caught fire, she was too frightened to let anyone know. However, Mother's sixth sense prompted her to look up the stairs. Nick, then seventeen years old, said he was the first one up the stairs but the heavy smoke stopped him. In the meantime his father rushed past him, pulled down the curtain, and in heavy smoke fought the fire. He told us that he was about to give up, when by the grace of God, he got the fire under control.

Over the years, the house witnessed many events. There was the whir of cream separator, the spinning wheel, the knitting machine, as well as the radio and family discussions, disagreements, teasing, and laughter. Some Sundays its walls vibrated as friends and neighbours gathered to sing hymns accompanied by the organ (I had purchased the organ while attending summer school in Edmonton). During the war it saw the concerns of parents and saw neighbours gather around the radio to hear Dad translate what was happening in Europe. The house absorbed the aromas of cooking and especially that of baking bread.

In time the house experienced a quiet period, except for days when grandchildren again filled it with the sounds of laughter.

Sadly, after many years it tired. It began to lean and sag. It would come down and give way to a small bungalow.

Chapter 4 My Grandparents—Who Were They?

My parents: Maria and Fred Bidulock, 1965.

When I was a child I did not know about grandparents. Except for aunts and uncles, there were no special older people who came to our house or whose houses we visited. Because grandparents were not part of my life, I did not miss them. As I grew older, I learned that everyone has four of them. But even though I must have had four as well, I was not aware of any of them.

The following account is information I gleaned from hearing my parents discuss instances in their lives involving their parents — my grandparents.

My maternal grandparents, Stefan and Sanfira, lived in Romania. But like many from that part of Europe, they too would venture forth to the New World.

A few years before Alberta became a province (1905), Stefan and Sanfira and their young family of five left their homeland for Canada. Their third child, Maria, who would later become my mother, was only five when they left. We know little of their homeland. At one time my mother told me that she thought that they came from Moldavia in Romania.

The ocean voyage across the Atlantic was long and tiring. The young family landed in Halifax and then took the long train trip to western Canada. Maria remembered little of the arduous trip from Europe to Alberta. The voyage must have been hard on the family, but especially on Sanfira.

Stefan applied for a homestead, but before he could build a house, winter approached. Despite the fact that he was a woodworker, he did not have the time to build a house. Consequently, the first winter was spent in a dugout, a hole dug in the side of a hill, with a roof of logs and clay to keep out the rain and snow. Mattresses of straw lined much of the floor.

Food was scarce, and before the family acquired a cow and chickens, much of their food was wildlife: grouse, ducks, fish, and sometimes rabbit. Stefan was often paid for his work with a sack of grain or a slab of pork. If my grandmother was anything like her daughter (my mother), she did without food for herself in order that her family was fed. But the harsh existence would take its toll on her.

Several years after arriving in Canada and living in poor conditions, Sanfira's health deteriorated. Was it influenza or pneumonia? No doctor was available to determine the cause of her death. Sanfira left her husband and a young family of five. The oldest was about twelve.

Stefan was devastated. Since he did carpentry work and was mostly away from home, he could not care for his young family. The children were put with strangers. Maria ended up with an English family near Hairy Hill. Her new family had two boys somewhat older than Maria. Maria's kindly manner and dedication grew on the family and they decided they wished to adopt her. As well, Maria liked her new family and home. She was glad to have a mother figure to teach her about the finer things in life. After learning English, as well as housekeeping and cooking, she was happy.

A couple of years later, just as she was starting to go to school, her father came to claim her. He wanted his family back together. And so Maria, at age eleven or twelve and still a child herself, looked after the other children in the family.

A widow from another district visited one afternoon. The children were alone while their father worked. When they got hungry they ground wheat between two special stones, mixed the resulting flour with water, and fried pancakes. They shared their meagre meal with the guest. She ate, left soon after, and never returned.

Stefan's gun was important to him. Many a meal depended on his marksmanship. But his gun would also be anything but a blessing.

As time passed, the family continued to subsist. Necessarily, the children became inventive and independent.

At eighteen, Maria met Fred (my father), a sinewy and brilliant young man of whom her father Stefan was not particularly fond. However, the match (made in heaven, I believe) blossomed and they married. It was after they were married and began a family that Stefan had a fatal accident. He was cleaning his gun. I do not know about cleaning guns, but it seems that to do a thorough job it was necessary to heat up the barrel. When Stefan pushed the end of the barrel into the stove, gunpowder that was still in the gun discharged. His thigh was shattered and he bled to death. So my maternal grandparents were gone before I was born. There were no pictures of them.

Who were Stefan and Sanfira? What did they look like? Did they have aspirations?

My mother had often mentioned Grandpa Stefan's red, curly hair. But in spite of the belief that people with red hair had a mean spirit, he had a kindly and mild manner. His sons, my uncles, were of medium height and build. I like to think he looked like them.

If Grandma Sanfira resembled her two daughters, she was short but made up for her stature with love and kindness. She prayed for her family as she suffered in silence.

I can only visualize what my mother's parents were like from the stories that my parents shared. I wish that I had known them.

My paternal grandparents, Helen and Paul, were strangers to me as well. I have not seen photos of them either.

Paul and Helen lived in Romania. They had four daughters and finally one son, Fred, who would later become my father. Life was difficult in Romania. Like his father (my great-grandfather) before him, Paul worked for a landlord. When Fred was a teenager, he was already following in his father's footsteps. He would never own land but he and his children, and their children, would work for landlords as his forefathers had done before him. One tenth of the farm produce was his pay. It was most difficult to feed a family with that arrangement.

News came from Canada from former neighbours who had lived under the same conditions before they had immigrated to Canada. In Canada they could get one quarter section of land (160 acres) for only the ten-dollar filing fee. To be a landowner was too good to be true. It was hardly imaginable. Fred and his oldest sister and her husband planned on immigrating to Canada. He was only sixteen. Fred dreamed of owning and working on his own land. He was tired of being awakened at 5:00 a.m. to clean barns and cut grain. He was young and adventurous.

So in about 1907 Fred was in a new country where there was the possibility that in a few years he could own his own land. That was his ultimate dream.

Helen, my grandmother, died in her homeland. A scratch or poke by a branch on her head became infected. The condition worsened and eventually took her life. It seems that Paul was somewhat reluctant to leave his homeland in spite of the difficult living conditions.

But Grandfather Paul and his other daughters did follow some time later. By the time they arrived, I believe that Fred had already applied for land.

Although the legal age for applying for land was 21, Fred applied when he was only nineteen, claiming he was of legal age. His intentions were honourable.

Paul lived for a while with his married children who had homesteads in the Deep Lake, Sandy Lake, and Moose Lake communities. Their dreams of living in the Boian area, named after the community in their homeland where they came from, did not come to pass. All homesteads in Boian had already been claimed.

Maternal grandparents Fred and Maria Bidulock with grandchildren Natalie, Charlene, Douglas, and Donald Murray, 1965.

As his children struggled to provide for their families, Paul decided to venture out on his own. He travelled north of the North Saskatchewan River and there found a new wife. He started a second family. Again he had four daughters, but Fred was his only son. It seems that he did not visit his children south of the river. He struggled to support a new family; the river was a natural barrier and he was elderly. Ties with his first family seemed broken.

I would have liked to have known my grandparents. Even photos would make thoughts of them more meaningful. Unfortunately cameras were not readily available in those times.

From the stories I heard from my parents, I can only admire my courageous grandparents and the difficult lives they endured. With faith and trust in God, they ventured into the unknown. They hoped that their struggles would make the lives of future generations easier.

Even though I did not know my grandparents, I must love them. I appreciate their sacrifices for me. I am part of their humble lives and I shall remember that all my life. I know that they were fine people because they were parents of my own dear parents.

Chapter 5 The Well

The well. Sketch, 2010.

During hot summer days, even though there may have been a full pail of water in the summerhouse, Mother often asked for fresh water. So after much pointing of fingers at one another, one member of the family took a pail and walked the rather long distance to the well. A bucket, fastened to the end of a rope that ran through a pulley, was lowered into the well. The bucket was then filled and drawn to the top, where it was poured into the pail and carried to the house.

Because there was no electricity in the area and therefore no refrigerator, during the hot summer, perishables like meat or cream were set into the bucket and lowered into the well, the rope firmly fastened to keep food just above the surface of the cool water.

Even though I saw my father "witching" or "divining" for water, I do not know if he used the method to locate the well that we used during our growing-up years.

When divining, Dad used a newly cut willow branch that had two tender twigs on its end. By holding a twig in each hand and allowing the end of the main branch to dangle, a "diviner" slowly moves across an area where he would like to have a well. He must possess a delicate sense of touch. Presumably, as he moves forward at a very slow pace, where underground water is present, he will feel the slightest suggestion of a pull or tug. The scientific explanation is that the willow, which thrives in wet areas, will want to seek the water. There were only one or two known diviners in our community. Not everyone has the gift.

When Dad dug his well, he built several wooden boxes with the tops and bottoms missing—sections of a crib to line the well with a framework of timber. Each crib section was three to four feet on each side. As digging by spade progressed to the depth of one crib section, another was lowered to prevent the sides from caving in. When digging progressed further, the previously positioned sections were pushed downward, and a new one added on top. Crib sections were added until the digging reached the water level. A final section was added on the surface with its top high enough to make for convenient handling of the pail. During the excavation, the digger filled buckets full of soil. One at a time each load was pulled up and emptied. Digging a well by hand was a slow and difficult process.

In Dad's well, water was found at approximately 15 feet—a shallow well. Digging had to stop sooner than expected because the digger hit a rock. However, there was enough room to dig a reservoir, a hole that allowed the water to collect. Dad claimed that our well was actually a spring. Water did not sit and stagnate. It always moved and so provided constant fresh water. Every few years a slender person was lowered into the well to clean out the reservoir because over time it filled with silt and sand. During the times when the well was being cleaned, water was collected prior to the commencement of the work—and stored for household use. If the water ran out before the work was completed, we took pails and walked through the pasture to a ravine near the river where we got good drinking water from a natural spring. The cows drank there all summer.

Dad built a wooden trough and supported it off the ground to prevent the bottom from rotting. It was situated near the well to supply water to the horses and cows during the winter.

On laundry days if the rain barrels were empty, water was hauled from the well.

During those early times Dad did not foresee a time when he might have running water in the house. But he could dream about it. In the mid-1960s when the old house was demolished and a bungalow built, his dream at last came true.

Chapter 6 A Singing Debut

Everyone knew that I was scheduled to sing. Stephen, our family friend and neighbour, knew. Mark, the local missionary, knew. My parents knew. Most of my siblings knew, especially my oldest sister Gladys, who was in her late teens, and my six-year-old sister Kathleen.

But I did not know.

Not much was shared with five-year-olds in our large farm family. The little ones were shadows in the background. We young kids could not compete with our older siblings. They assumed centre stage with their jokes, or fascinating stories about how they ran into a bear and survived to tell the story, or how they escaped the squirts of a skunk. We younger children admired the heroes of the tall tales, but we remained unheard.

During the Depression, our parents welcomed missionaries, like Mark, who visited our homestead. Messages of hope and love were an inspiration to our family. We attended the "Sunday School" sessions held in nearby country schools.

Our neighbour, Stephen, lived across the lake from us in a small cabin set deep in dense woods. He was somewhat of a recluse. Farming did not interest him, but books did. He could not afford to continue formal education after completing eighth grade at our one-room country school. Instead he became a self-taught scholar. Somewhere and somehow he acquired books: medical books, science books, history books, and the Bible. He studied the Bible extensively and enjoyed discussing religion with Mark and other missionaries who visited in the area.

The summer I was five, Stephen visited at our homestead often. He was in his mid-twenties, handsome, with a fair complexion and a kindly disposition. The purpose of Stephen's visits was twofold. First, he loved to listen to Kathleen and me sing simple hymns; but he also cast affectionate glances towards my sister Gladys.

One Sunday morning Gladys gave Kathleen and me a thorough scrubbing. She fussed over our hair.

I wished Mother would let us wear bangs, like the girls at school. But when we asked she said, "Bangs are for horses. I'd like you girls to part your hair on one side and comb it to the other."

Consequently, my hair fell over one eye most of the time.

Ribbons, a scarce item in those days, were located in Gladys's secret shoebox hidden under her bed. That morning she fashioned bows, and fastened them to our hair. After many trips to the wood stove to exchange irons, she pressed our pink dresses to her liking. We looked like twins because our mother made the two dresses out of one bolt of material. It was cheaper and faster that way.

Gladys dusted off our black patent leather shoes. They were of patchwork leather. The T. Eaton Company manufactured them from leftover pieces of leather. But they were special to us. I remember my mother saying, "Those shoes cost a *whole* seventy-five cents a pair! You girls can wear them *only* on special occasions, and be *sure* to keep them clean!"

My feet had obviously grown since the last special occasion. After much pushing and squeezing, I finally managed to get them on.

Gladys stepped back and looked at us with admiration. Every now and then she readjusted the bows in our hair, or fluffed the narrow skirts of the dresses. Her theory was *If a girl looks pretty, that is all that matters.*

I did not know what all the fuss was about until Gladys stepped back one more time, cocked her head to one side, smiled, and said, "Oh, that's nice! But remember to smile when you sing."

Ah, we were going to sing. But where? And for whom?

Stephen walked through the gate and knocked at the open door. He smiled at Gladys approvingly, then remarked, "They are lovely."

Then he called to Kathleen and me, "I'm sorry but we'll have to hurry. I don't want Missionary Mark to wait for us. Come on, girls. Let's go."

At a quick pace we headed towards the barn and then west through the wooded pasture. The worn path was familiar to me. The cows came home for milking on that path. There to our left was the large, flat rock that Kathleen and I had dubbed a "restaurant," even though we had never been to a real one. When our tin cups were filled with wild strawberries, we would climb on top of the rock and pretend we were in a "restaurant."

When we approached the westerly side of our homestead and crossed onto our neighbour's land, the path became less distinct and walking more difficult. We proceeded along the brow of the ravine, parallel to the North Saskatchewan River. Branches of aspen, birch, diamond willow, and high bush cranberry sprawled across the seldom-used trail. Stephen, who was in the lead, often held the branches high for us. Kathleen, who followed him closely, fared well, but as he released the branches they slapped me in the face or threw me off balance. The twigs tugged at my hair.

Kathleen turned to coax me on. "Hurry," she urged, "and why are you crying?"

"I'm not crying," I answered. "A branch went in my eye." Then I failed to see a broken branch lying near the path. It stuck into me like a dagger. "Oooh," I groaned quietly, and felt wetness trickle down my bare leg. With a quick swish of my hand, the sticky mess was smoothed down. But I had to press on. We were late, and I was falling behind. I ran.

Although I was aware of discomfort to my feet, I did not realize that I was developing blisters on my heels. I limped on, rubbing my smarting eye and

Approach to Desjarlais Ferry. Watercolour, 1985.

smearing the blood down my leg. "When will this end," I wondered. But I was afraid to ask.

I was near complete exhaustion, and about to collapse, when we emerged from the dark woods and crossed a small farmyard to a dirt road. Near the end of the road, on the top of a hill that sloped down towards the river, was a small building with a dark car parked beside it. During the Depression, cars were rarely seen in our community, so I was surprised.

The young man standing near the car noticed our arrival. He hurried towards us, then smiled and extended his hand to Stephen. A hearty handshake was followed by a friendly slap on the back. Immediately his gaze was diverted to my sister and me. He took a long, hard look at me. His face lacked emotion. I rubbed a grubby hand across my hot face and tried to brush away the hair that fell over my eye.

"How far did you walk?" Missionary Mark asked.

"Well, it was two miles through heavy bush," Stephen answered. "We tried to hurry, but it was hard going."

"The ferry is on its way over to this side. We have a few minutes. Come with me." Mark led the way into the small shop.

"I am so thirsty," I whispered to Kathleen. She looked around and then pointed to a bucket of water that was set on a wooden crate. I filled the dipper and drank. Then I took a deep breath and drank again. It was so refreshing.

Mark stood near a small counter. He dug into his pocket and picked three nickels from the few coins in the palm of his hand. That was a lot of money, I thought. I did not think my father had that much money. The lady waiting on him smiled and gave him three chocolate bars, which he promptly distributed to us.

We got into the car and slowly descended the steep slope to the Desjarlais ferry. It had already docked. Crossing the river on the ferry was a new experience. As I took in the wonder of it all, I heard my sister tearing the wrapper off her chocolate bar. She was eating her chocolate! How could she! The precious gift was too important to eat so soon. It was the first chocolate bar I ever had. No! I will save mine as long as possible. I might even share it with my little brother when we get home. George would love it. Mother would enjoy a bite too. Yes, I must save my chocolate bar. I held it safely in my hot little hand.

Once on the other side of the river, Mark drove the car up the incline from the ferry and along the narrow road. He chatted with Stephen. Their conversation was gentle and soothing. I felt comfortable and content as I sat in the back seat with my sister.

Eventually we pulled into the Hamlin school playground. The folks who had gathered there greeted Missionary Mark with warmth. In the schoolhouse, Stephen asked us to sit in a double desk, at the front of the classroom. My chocolate bar felt sticky but it was safe in my hands, which rested in my lap.

After a few hymns and scripture reading, Mark announced that my sister and I would sing "Jesus Loves the Little Children." Timidly and still clinging to my chocolate bar, I followed Kathleen to the front of the room. We sang:

> "Jesus loves the little children
> All the children of the world
> Red or yellow, black or white,
> All are precious in His sight.
> Jesus loves the little children of the world."

We were soon in Mark's car on our way home. When I heard Mark tell Stephen that he would drive the extra six miles to take us home, I kicked off my shoes. The blisters on my heels had burst and smarted. It was a relief to be in bare feet again, even though Gladys would not approve.

We arrived home, hungry and tired. Mother was on her way to the house with an armful of vegetables from the garden. "Please stay and share dinner with us," she invited. Both men gladly accepted.

Gladys hurried out of the summerhouse to greet Mark and Stephen.

"They sang beautifully," Mark reported happily. "The folks out at Hamlin just loved them and would like the girls back any time."

My big sister was pleased and then her gaze fell on me. Her jaw dropped. She looked horrified.

"Pearl," she shrieked. "What has happened to you? Why are you barefoot? What is that mess on your leg? Your face is dirty. Your hair is a mess! Where is the bow I put in your hair?"

Stephen tried to ease the situation. "It's adorning a branch near the path we took to the ferry. It's the most beautiful tree in the forest," he teased. But Gladys was not amused, nor was she finished.

"What is that dirty mess on the front of your dress? Was it there when you sang in front of all those people?"

A wooded shortcut to the ferry, 1990.

I looked down and for the first time noticed the brown smears on my pink dress. I retreated towards the barn.

"Come, George," I called to my little brother and took his hand. "Come. I have something really good."

We squatted near the building and absorbed the rays of the setting sun. I tugged at the torn and soggy paper wrapped around the soft chocolate. We poked our fingers into the thick brown syrup and then licked them clean. It was delicious. The lambs, chickens, and turkeys approached and watched with curiosity.

After fingers and wrapping were licked clean, I looked at George. He had brown smears on his mouth and face. A brown spot on his eyelid bobbed up and down.

"George," I asked, "does Jesus love brown children too?"

My two-year-old brother nodded his head up and down. "Yup," he replied. Then in a high soprano he sang, "Jesus 'wovs' me. This I know. I know. I know. I know . . ."

And the world was at peace.

We watched the sunset and the world was at peace. Oil, 1960.

Chapter 7 The Early Garden

A large garden fed a large family. 1945.

During the "dirty thirties," potatoes in the root cellar meant that the family would not starve that winter. Potatoes were the homesteaders' most important vegetable. They kept well in root cellars. It was important to have enough to last the winter for food and also for the following spring's seeding. At planting time each potato was cut in half or thirds. It was necessary that each section planted had at least one *eye* for new growth to occur.

Generally a large area was planted on the edge of the field west of the lake. I recall one year when potatoes were planted beyond the lake on the edge of a field that had been inundated with Canada thistles. Dad decided that the planting, hoeing, and "hilling" would rid the area of the horrid weed. Weed killers were not yet known. The plan failed because the garden was far from home and did not get the constant weeding required. The thistles interfered with the growth of the potatoes. That year we had bushels of tiny potatoes. They were often washed and boiled in their skins rather than peeled.

Netted gems were the only variety of potato grown in the community. However, by 1950, Mother acquired a red variety and several years later, she was introduced to yellow banana potatoes. The bananas were her favourites. After a few years of planting them next to the red variety, she noticed that the bananas took on a red hue. She took steps to correct that.

Banana potatoes were generally cooked in their skins. The skin was peeled before dipping them into a garlic sauce. Although it was very tasty, one remained at home after that meal.

Beets, turnips, and carrots were also stored in the cellar but unlike the potatoes, they rarely kept well until spring.

Very few seeds were bought in those days. A few peas and beans were allowed to mature on the vine and then used as seeds the following spring. Cabbages were also grown in large numbers. The cabbage seeds and carrot seeds were bought at the G.M. (George Michalcheon) General Store in Hairy Hill, twelve miles away. Seeds were often kept from year to year. Tomato seeds were also saved from over-ripe tomatoes. At least one cucumber was left on the vine to mature until it turned yellow and the seeds harvested, but most seeds for cucumbers were bought. I do not recall lettuce or spinach in our garden. Those vegetables were unknown in the early days. Pumpkin vines crawled over other vegetables and grew well.

I remember long rows of hemp plants along the potato patch. The seeds were harvested, flailed, and chaff was removed by pouring them from one container into another on a windy day. In the winter the seeds were taken to a farmer who owned a press and were converted into flavourful oil quite comparable to olive oil. After the growing of hemp was banned, some farmers grew it secretly in the middle of a field of grain. They did it for the oil. But helicopters and planes easily spotted the rich green patches.

Horseradish root dug in the early spring was mild and palatable. One homesteader had horseradish on the edge of a wheat field and it spread. To destroy it, the farmer decided to plough it up. Instead of destroying it he had a new row of plants where the plough tore and dragged it.

I think that dill was the only herb grown. Its seeds and leaves were a must for canning pickles. When doing pickles, Mother cut tender branches off pin-cherry trees and added them to the pickles. A wild variety of sage grew near the gate but I do not recall it being used in cooking.

Maria's Bounty. Pastel, 1975.

Although each summer we picked wild strawberries and wild, somewhat wormy raspberries, in later years the domestic varieties found a place in our garden and were a welcomed change. For a while we also had gooseberries and currants.

As Mother aged, she foresaw difficulties in going down the ravines by the river for high bush cranberries so she transplanted tender shoots near the lake, at the bottom of the garden. They did not yield as well as in their natural habitat. But Mother often tried out things like that. She experimented with seeds from apples, watermelon, and other fruit that was bought. Sometimes it worked and other times it didn't. She would find out. In her own right, she was a great researcher.

About the only garden tools available were hoes made by Dad. He used old disc plates that were broken while disking rocky fields. The hole in the centre of the plate held the handmade wooden handle in place. Only about one third of each disc was used for one hoe. He cut it, leaving points on each of the two ends. The hoe was far superior to any hoe found in garden shops because the pointed ends easily cut weeds near the good plants.

Seeds and perennials, including flowers, were often shared by the women in the community. Gardens were generally large and required much weeding, hoeing, and harvesting, but were very necessary to keep the family fed. We were happy and content when the last potato was dropped down the small chute, on the west side of the house, to the cellar.

As the children grew, they were required to help maintain the garden. Over time, most members of the family developed a love for gardening, which proves an old saying: . . . *those who work with soil are near to God.*

Chapter 8 Mother, M.D.

Family photo, 1934. Top Row: Gladys, Mike, Dan, Helen, John. Middle Row: Nick, Steve. Front Row: Kathleen, Maria and baby Lucille, little George, Fred, Pearl. Insets: Adeline and Bertha – arrived later.

At our family farm, injury and illness were healed with time, by nature, and by the grace of God. That was what my mother believed in. She examined each health concern and quickly decided if it warranted her time of day. As a rule, Mother let nature take its course, but occasionally, she took sudden and drastic action.

Because we ran around the barnyard and through the woods in bare feet, bruises and scrapes were common. If infection set in, Mother took extra notice and the infected limb was introduced to "soaking."

Fevers were diagnosed with the touch of her hand, and were treated with cold compresses and lots of lemonade.

Head colds did not usually last long, so Mother was not overly concerned when one of her flock got the sniffles. Unbeknownst to either her or us, our colds were treated by the high humidity experienced on laundry day. The stove was covered with every pot and pan Mom owned. They held melting snow, which was heated for the waiting washtub and scrub board. We leaned over the wood-burning cast-iron stove for warmth, breathing the gentle steam as it bathed our faces and unclogged our nostrils and sinuses.

The only purchased medicine in our home was a big red can of Watkins' ointment. The salve was used for both man and animal. The whole family depended on it, at least when it was available. At other times, improvisation was called for.

For example, although my brother regularly swam in Sandy Lake with no side effects, one time he developed an extremely itchy skin condition. Fearing that the rash was contagious, Mother concocted her own medicine. She was out of the cure-all Watkins' salve and could not wait for the Watkins man to come around again. This was an emergency!

The three main ingredients she used were pinesap, honey, and sulphur. She added little bits of this and that, to make a sticky black ointment. From head to toe each family member was smeared with the gooey mess. The itchy rash took flight.

Mother's ultimate tampering with medicine took place after a man visited the farm, claiming he could help women who had varicose veins and discomfort in their legs. He showed Mother the leaves of the plant he used in the healing process. He would charge one dollar to treat her left leg.

Perhaps she could not spare the money or perhaps she felt uncomfortable with the idea of a strange man touching her leg. Regardless of the reason, she declined his offer. She had, however, recognized the leaves he showed her. So, the following day, she found the plant growing near our lake and decided to undertake her own treatment. That night she layered the leaves around the calf of her leg, wrapping them with a flannelette diaper to keep everything in place. Then she went to bed.

During the night a burning sensation woke her. She quickly removed the poultice.

In the morning, a large blister covered Mother's leg from knee to ankle. Mother bound it because she thought the liquid in the blister would promote healing, even though the weight threatened to burst it.

About a week later, Mother took her regular catnap after lunch. She removed the bandage in order to expose her leg to the air. While she slept we heard dripping sounds and noticed water under the edge of the cot.

"Mother, are you peeing your bed?" my sister called out.

The blister had burst but healing had already begun. Time, nature, and God had helped. Thereafter, the treated leg was her strong leg. The treatment had worked. She learned later that proper timing would have saved much discomfort. The experience, however, did not deter her from practising and experimenting with medicine. Not my mother!

Chapter 9 The Lake

A landscape of peace and tranquillity. Watercolour, 1970.

Probably the most calming aspect of the landscape was the presence of water. The chorus of geese honking and flapping their wings on the shore, the mallards, and the smaller waterfowl were always present. In the late summer a heron regularly visited our lake. It always stopped in the same location, and like a statue, stood on one leg for long periods of time. In the fall, hunters occasionally came to our lake. They generally asked Dad for permission to hunt. Dad reluctantly agreed but he himself did not wish to kill wildlife just for sport. In time, the hunters got the message as fewer turned up.

Aerial view of the farm and lake, 1940.

When the lake froze, we sometimes shovelled off a strip of snow for skating or just sliding. Occasionally young people in the community joined us. Few youngsters owned skates. But Mike, the inventor, nailed a strip of metal between two pieces of wood. He fastened these to the bottom of his boots—and skated! His design was copied by other ambitious folk.

During my growing years, I remember the lake being there at all times. However, it underwent a major change that had Dad concerned.

During the early years each homesteader was required to do road improvements in lieu of taxes: one day per year per farm. Each farmer provided an operator, a team of horses, and a "fresno" or "slip" (a metal scoop to move soil). Years later the municipality acquired road-building machines, and the farmers were no longer required to participate.

One summer a truckload of gravel was dumped and packed down into a low spot on the road that circled the lake. The procedure, like a dam, stopped the natural underground flow of water from the lake, and so Dad's lake grew larger and larger and flooded much of the grazing area around it. Dad was most unhappy, but his complaints went unheeded.

Spruce trees planted by John in front of the lake, 1980.

In the last two decades the lake situation took a drastic turn in the opposite direction. The water table had dropped and the lake that was part of our life disappeared. In time the larger lake dried up too. I miss the water that was so much a part of my childhood.

Chapter 10 The West Quarter

Winter on the farm. Pastel, 1973.

Our western neighbour had a poor homestead. The southern part of his land had hills and rocks. Machinery was constantly breaking. The land was not suitable for cultivation. The northern half consisted of deep ravines that ran to the river. The only positive aspect of that homestead was a creek that provided water for animals.

Although his intentions were honourable, our neighbour could not sustain

Stooks near creek on the west quarter. Watercolour, 1980.

Granaries on the east (home) quarter. Watercolour, 1980.

his family on such poor land. Eventually he sold the land to Dad for $500. Dad used it mostly for hay and pasture.

When our neighbours were about to leave, his wife invited Mother to get raspberry plants from her garden. Until that time we had picked only wild raspberries. Our mother, Helen, and I got the plants. They produced large berries on tall plants—a real blessing. Those raspberries were not wormy like the wild ones; they were large and juicy. A favourite dessert of raspberries topped with fresh farm cream had family members smacking their lips.

Mother planted the tall bushes along the garden fence for support. The mother plants, the first generation, found their spot in Mother's garden during the "dirty thirties." But other generations followed. First they grew in children's gardens and later in gardens of grandchildren. As well, baby plants that sprouted in unwanted places were gladly given away to anyone who wanted them. Mother's raspberries have emigrated to other provinces in our country where, I suspect, they continue to multiply and reach new gardens.

Chapter 11 "E" Stands for Eaton's

In the early 1900s new Eastern European immigrants had little or no knowledge of the English language and few opportunities to learn. Newspapers were rarely available. Television had not yet been invented. The scant world news reaching the community did so via the grapevine or crystal radio sets, with verbal translations by the few bilingual neighbours.

However, there was one readily available and constant source of "English as a Second Language" education: the Eaton's catalogue. With the help of their children, who were learning English in school, and the pictures in the Eaton's catalogue, the new immigrants began to understand the language of their adopted home.

The Eaton's catalogue advertised everything: hats and spats, coats, dresses, men's suits, underwear, bloomers, fabric, toys, books, household goods; you name it—Eaton's had it. Shoes included sandals, loafers, pumps, galoshes, leather boots, felt boots, cowboy boots, rubber boots, and more. Cloth was available in muslin, print, corduroy, denim, linen, silk, and wool.

Through Eaton's, the new Canadians learned about order forms, money orders, and C.O.D.s (cash on delivery).

The catalogue served as a fashion magazine too. The girls studied the pages full of models—the dresses, the shoes, the hairstyles, and even the stances—as they dreamed of wearing the clothes they could not afford. Young men admired the men's wear: the shiny black shoes, the double-breasted suits, the hats that portrayed masculinity.

Two large Eaton's catalogues were expected each year: one for summer and one for winter. When a new catalogue arrived in the mail, the old one was retired to the outhouse, where it continued to serve as a fashion magazine, as well as toilet tissue. Generally, the back index pages were torn out first, followed by the other less desirable sections. When a young family member was late for dinner or shirking chore responsibilities, he was likely perusing the big book while sitting on the throne.

In our community, Deep Lake, the T. Eaton Company and the post office were trusted and held in high regard. Our post office was operated by Mr. Shalka

"S" stands for Singer, 2003.

and the district was ultimately named after him. An order taken in for the Tuesday or Saturday morning mail pick-up resulted in the arrival of a parcel precisely one week later. It never failed.

Eaton's service proved honest and fair. If merchandise was out of stock, it was substituted with an item of equal or better quality. If it cost less than the article ordered, the difference was made in coupons—soft green coupons, which were used to pay for future orders.

At the age of four, I too became indebted to Eaton's for kick-starting my early education.

It all happened on an extremely cold winter's day. Dad and the older boys decided not to cut trees that day for the next year's supply of firewood. It was just too cold! Besides, Mother could use their help indoors. A wool quilt was nearing completion, and had reached the stage where Father's help was important.

The previous spring, the wool had been shorn off the sheeps' backs. That summer, when the rain barrels overflowed with soft water, the wool was washed in several soapy baths, rinsed, and laid out to dry. The clean dry wool was stored under a bed until the winter came. Then during the long cold evenings, our family sat together in the large kitchen/living/dining room, pulling the wool to loosen the fibres. The soft and fluffy mass was then carded into batts, which were layered between two sheets of cotton print and loosely hand-basted together. Rather than take the time to hand-quilt, the assembly was sewn securely together by machine. At that stage, many hands were needed to hold the bulky quilt level with the sewing machine.

Father stood behind the treadle, directly in line with the needle, pulling just enough to guide the stitching. Mother sat in front of the machine, pumping the treadle, while feeding the quilt through. The other available family members held the quilt up to prevent it from flopping and sagging. It would take most of the day! After the first few lengths of stitching, the chore proved boring for a four-year-old like me.

I pretended to help, but mostly rubbed my face on the soft fluffy wool. The lingering fragrance of lanolin was nice. Later, I sat on the floor under the wool canopy, watching Mother's foot tirelessly pumping the machine. This was a private place. I liked private places.

The aroma of cooking chicken filled the room. For lunch, Mother would remove the boiled meat from the hot water and sauté it in sour cream. Vegetables were added to the broth for soup. The smells made me hungry.

My canopy disappeared as the quilt was gently rolled up and set on a cot. The stitching would continue after lunch. The sewing machine was rolled from the centre of the room towards its permanent spot near a window. A small nook was created. The spot was enclosed on four sides by the wall, the sofa, the desk, and the sewing machine. I crawled over the treadle into the secret enclave. It felt good to be alone.

I pulled Father's bulky sweater from the couch, using it as a rug on the cold floor. I stood up and explored my surroundings. Mother's big shiny scissors lay on the top of the sewing machine. I reached for them, knelt down, and tried them. They were too big for my small hands and there was nothing nearby to practise my cutting on. I stood up again. On the windowsill were four soft green papers. They were nice. They were beautiful. Each had a large diamond shape with a symbol in its centre, as well as a border of tiny diamonds along its outer edge. Now, I planned, if I could cut out each diamond, I might use them on the checkerboard for a special game. I took the green papers and ducked down again.

The scissors were too big to handle easily. I would have to use both hands.

All the big diamond shapes would be cut first. The cuts were sloppy. The paper bent between the cutting blades. I concentrated. Then I jumped as an anxious voice called, "What are you doing?"

My sister Helen pushed the sewing machine just enough to get into my private nook. She knelt beside me.

"You shouldn't cut these. They are Eaton's coupons. They're like money. We can send them to Eaton's to buy things." She guided my index finger and traced the symbol in the big diamond shape. One vertical stroke and three horizontal branches.

"This is 'E.' See," she pointed out. "And 'E' stands for Eaton's." She pointed to numbers on the coupon—fifteen cents, eight cents, twenty-four cents, twelve cents. "This money is half of a pair of shoes for you. It can buy one shoe."

"Why would anyone want one shoe?" I wondered.

Helen mixed flour and water and pasted the coupons onto a sheet of paper. "Maybe Eaton's will take these. But don't ever do that again."

The "E"'s in the diamond shapes looked curious. I was about to crawl out from under the sewing machine, when I noticed a snake-shaped symbol on the machine. I traced it with my finger.

"What's this, Helen?" I asked.

"That's an 'S.' 'S' stands for Singer. See the S-I-N-G-E-R? That spells Singer. It's the company that made the machine. And your name starts with 'P.'"

My formal learning had begun, and there was no looking back.

Chapter 12 The Radio

Father liked to listen to the news—especially during the Second World War, 2003.

The day Harry demonstrated and then sold Father a special radio changed our lives forever.

Until the 1930s, news at the homesteads was reported by mouth. We looked forward to visitors because there was always some bit of news that our parents later discussed. I liked that.

I remember a Maytag salesman who came to our house to show Mother a gasoline-operated wringer washer. The appliance would reduce the workload on laundry day. During his sales pitch, he casually mentioned the death of King George V.

"It's too bad. I didn't know that he wasn't well. He was a fine man," I heard Father say sadly.

When our parents went to town, often by buggy, they returned with outdated world news they had heard in Hairy Hill. But that would change.

John and Mike, who were in their late teens and also interested in mechanics, had heard about crystal set radios. They researched and obtained the necessary parts to build one.

During the summer the big house was mainly used for sleeping. The family congregated and ate in the summerhouse. One special Sunday afternoon, however, John and Mike invited one family member at a time to experience their invention in the quiet of the big house. When my turn came I became very curious because other members of the family returned excited and surprised.

Earphones were placed over my head. I was asked to be very quiet because they claimed the aerial was inadequate. A long, tall aerial would catch the radio waves more effectively.

I held my breath as voices came through the earphones. The sounds came from a radio station in Edmonton and the radio waves came through the air. That was too much for me to understand.

As the crystal set became a household item, the novelty wore off. Father liked to listen to the news "on the hour" while resting in the evening with a thin hand-rolled cigarette.

As radios became more available, we bought a little battery-operated radio. However, if we played it all day, the batteries soon lost their energy. I remember Father coming into the house and saying, "Turn that music off. The batteries will die and we won't get the news."

But the songs by Wilf Carter, Johnny Cash, and the Carter family included music too beautiful to turn off. So we turned the volume down and put our ears close to the radio. Less energy would be used if the volume was down, and should Father come in unexpectedly he would not be aware of our crime.

One evening, Harry, a friend and salesman, brought a large radio to our house. It looked like an elegant piece of furniture, made of fine wood. It stood more than a metre high. On the face of it were cut out scrolls to allow the sound to come through. Above that was a dial that contained two lines. One line had numbers on it; the other had two words: *short wave*. There were three knobs: one for locating stations, one for volume, and the third for short wave. Father often talked to friends and neighbours about the short wave, but I did not know what it meant. Every now and then he excitedly announced at breakfast that around midnight the previous evening he got Sacramento, or Spokane or Des Moines. One morning he told us that he thought he had received Europe. He had heard faint German voices.

Much of the good reception was credited to a good aerial: a wire suspended from the top of a tall pole attached to one corner of the house. It ran the length of the yard to another tall pole.

In spite of the special radio, the battery problem still existed. The community had not yet been hooked up to electricity. Batteries were the energy required to run radios. Again we were cautioned not to listen to silly music. Energy must be saved for news time.

Instead of buying new batteries every time the old ones were dead, Father would recharge them. He built a small windmill and fastened it to the top of the summerhouse. Since roads became impassable in the wintertime and the car was stored for the winter months, Father removed the car batteries and recharged them using a generator attached to the windmill. We used these and any extra car batteries to power the radio. When the batteries were dead, we prayed for wind.

Second World War news had Father's ear glued to the radio every evening. His oldest son, John, was overseas serving with the RCAF. Father would keep track of the events going on in Europe. Now neighbours who did not have radios often spent evenings around our big radio. They too were interested in learning about the war. Some of their sons served in the armed forces but except for John, all trained in Canada and none sailed across the Atlantic.

For a couple of decades, before the telephone and electricity reached our community, the big radio was our constant connection with the outside world. Father often remembered Harry, who had helped change our secluded lives.

The radio was an important addition to our household. It reported the time every hour. It kept us aware of world news, and we enjoyed the lovely music of that era. Radios were wonderful inventions and forerunners of greater future technology.

Chapter 13 Dad's First Thresher

Pitching sheaves into the thresher, 1950.

I remember my father's first threshing machine. It was the first thresher in the community and many neighbours depended on it to thresh their grain.

Its inner mechanism had the usual chompers and beaters which most threshers have. But the parts of the exterior that could be seen easily were primitive compared to later models. The machine had a long low table at the front of it to accommodate an engine.

Although at that time horses were invaluable, they could not do the engine's work. Father's engine was like a best friend. It was important for three special jobs. By connecting it to a saw, in a day or two it prepared the winter's supply of firewood. It also ran the grain grinder. Generally, before threshing time began, Father spent a whole day grinding enough grain to last throughout the threshing season. The engine's third and most important job was to run the thresher.

Fred standing beside thresher, 1970.

With two pieces of wood about one foot long and an old mower blade fastened between them at one end, Dad designed the knife for the person who stood on the table in front of the thresher feeder. There were no pulleys to guide the sheaves as in later threshers. A person in front of the feeder cut the twine with a quick chop. The sheaf was then slowly and evenly pushed into the mouth of the monster. As well, whereas later models had blowers to blow the straw to a pile a fair distance from the machine, the first thresher had a steep ten- to fifteen-foot ramp at the back that folded in the middle during transport. When it was stretched out and up during threshing, a chain pulley drew the straw to its top, from where

Pitching hay onto the hayrack. Pastel, 1975.

it flopped over onto the ground below. When the straw pile became as high as the top of the ramp, a "straw man" was required to pull the straw away. I recall Gladys doing the job when I was little. I climbed the pile to help, but soon left.

The machine was moved from farm to farm with horses. The farmer plus other farmers who would be involved supplied a crew. Racks brought in the sheaves and unloaded them to the feeder, spike pitchers stayed on the field to help load the racks, and, when a wagon was full of grain, a person took it to the granary and unloaded it with a grain shovel—by hand, of course. Dad looked after the oiling of the machine and saw to its smooth running.

Often while a farmer helped as part of the threshing crew, his wife and older children brought sheaves off their fields to a location where they wanted their straw pile and stacked the sheaves. It was important to stack dry sheaves with the grain end towards the middle. In that way, even if inclement weather came, the grain was protected because it was in the middle. Also, if it snowed, Dad was still able to thresh the grain right from the stacks. Sometimes he did not get home until near Christmas.

Fred's first mechanical help—a portable engine, 1932.

Harvesting continued until sundown. Watercolour, 1970.

While Dad was away, it was necessary for Mother to prepare for winter with the help of the older children. I remember her saying that she was so glad when he finally got home. Most often Dad was paid not in currency but with a few sacks of grain.

In later years when threshers were improved, and other farmers invested in them, Dad, with the older children helping, preferred it to be a family project. He liked working for himself on his own time.

Harvesting the old way was hard work but in many ways it was good. A pile of straw was a fine place for cows to feed and sleep all winter. Memories of a stooked field linger with me. Times have changed, but the hard work of the old harvest methods is a wonderful memory.

Chapter 14 Why I Don't Eat Eggs

"No, thank you." I pass the eggs on and under my breath say, "No eggs for me." Poached eggs, fried eggs, hard-boiled, scrambled—I refuse to look at them and so do not see them. They are not for me. I have no interest in eggs.

Eggs are healthy. They provide protein to our diet. They are a universal food. So why not eat them? It happened a long, long time ago. I was little more than a toddler.

Natalie Murray by old chicken coop, 1959.

Natalie Murray directs Grandma's chickens, 1959.

When I was five, I looked up to our dad. I looked way, way up—more than six feet up. He was tall. He was smart. He knew everything. In my young years I felt that everything that he did was always right.

One summer day my sister Kathleen and I were playing near the sheep barn. We found a nest with three eggs in it and were surprised that the hen did not lay the eggs in the hen house. After all, she was infringing on the sheeps' area. That was not right. We would tell our mother about our discovery.

In the meantime I picked up one egg and studied it. I turned it around and around. It was a beautiful egg. So round; so smooth; so shiny. Then I thought of our dad. He would appreciate that particular egg. He was a smart man. Why did not others in our family copy Father's example? Because they were not smart like he was. But I would be smart like him.

Upon rising and before he went out to check on the animals, our dad often chose an egg from a basket on the sideboard. He carefully knocked one end; just enough to break the shell on the very end. He picked the shell to make a nice round hole and expose its contents. With a quick backward tilt of his head, he emptied its contents down his throat. He smacked his lips, ran his arm across his mouth, reached for his coat, and left for the outdoors. He would return later for the porridge that Mother would cook for the family.

We rarely had eggs for breakfast. Breakfast at our house was generally porridge and quite often pancakes too. Mother made the best pancakes in the world. She used an egg or two and buttermilk or curdled milk that was intended for homemade cheese. The eggs in her batter were lost in the beating. I did not see them. Her fluffy, thick pancakes fried in homemade butter could not be beat. In later years when I left home, I recall having pancakes in special pancake restaurants. They were thin, limp, and tasteless compared to those we had at the farm.

One could possibly credit it to the fresh farm produce, including the fresh eggs.

Back at the sheepfold, I showed the favourite egg to my sister.

"Let's drink these like Dad does," I suggested. Kathleen was not sure about that. She slowly shook her head.

"I don't know how to do it. You go first."

"Okay," I responded bravely. I knocked the end of the egg on a post. It remained intact. A hard rock would be better. When it was done, the egg looked half crushed.

"That's all right. I know how to fix it." Next the shell was removed until the yellow yolk looked at me as if to defy me.

"Okay." With head tilted back like I saw Father do, I emptied the contents into my mouth. Slimy egg white and yellow yolk filled my mouth, covered my face, and dripped down my dress. I gagged. I spluttered. I spat.

"Yuk. Yuk. Yuk." It was no use pretending to be brave. The experience was most disgusting.

"I don't like it," I admitted timidly. "And don't you tell anyone!"

Since that fateful day when I was five, I have eaten eggs only when I did not see them; that is, if they were lost in cake batter or other foods.

Chapter 15 Homesteaders and the Spanish Flu

Father goes across snowy terrain to help a neighbour. Watercolour, 1975.

While watching a documentary about the Spanish flu that attacked the world in 1918, I recalled stories my father told us regarding that period.

It was estimated that more than 40 million people throughout the world succumbed to the dreadful scourge. Before the flu hit our country, about 30,000 Canadians had lost their lives in the First World War and ironically, about the same number of Canadians later died of the flu. The documentary stated that these types of pandemics occur in cycles and that the world is well overdue for another one.

Canadian soldiers returned at the end of the war, some maimed and crippled, but all happy to be back home in a safe place. Many, however, later died of the flu.

Because ships from Europe landed in eastern Canada, that part of the country was hit first. But with train travel, the disease moved west. Deaths were numerous. In some instances, especially in Winnipeg, mass graves were required to keep up with the burials.

The flu did not begin in Spain, as is erroneously believed. Because that country was the first to report it in a newspaper, it was regarded as the *Spanish* flu.

At that time Dad was a young homesteader with his wife and four young children: John, Gladys, Mike, and a new baby, Dan. The pandemic was frightening.

Because the homesteaders were relatively isolated, one would think that they would not have been exposed to the disease. But they were.

Dad's west neighbours were sick. In spite of the danger, he felt obliged to help. With food that his wife prepared tucked under his arm, he walked in snow through woods, across hills, ravines, and a spring and finally made a steep climb to his neighbours' home. Before he reached the house he stopped and tied a thick cloth over his mouth and nose. He knocked and then opened the door just enough to push the food through. In a muffled voice he inquired about their health. He was aware of a strong garlic odour. He stacked firewood near the door and cared for the few animals. Then hurriedly, as if to escape a monster, he retraced his steps to his home and family. A similar routine continued for several days. The precautions he exercised likely helped keep his family healthy.

There were relatively few deaths in the neighbourhood. Many believed that wearing beads made with garlic cloves both prevented the illness from attacking and helped those who were already ill. Medicines and vaccines did not exist so homesteaders relied on their instincts. Garlic seemed like a good remedy.

So with the help of God, garlic and Fred, our neighbours survived the Spanish flu.

Chapter 16 Wool, Wool, Wonderful Wool

Knitting machine, interestingly called "Money Maker." Photo, 2003.

How far does a fleece of wool go? In my estimation, my mother explored every possible facet.

During the month of June, when the snow had long disappeared and the spring sun approached the equinox, the sheep at the homestead were eager to donate their fleeces to any cause my mother could think of, as long as it would soon be removed from their backs. They spent their resting time sleeping in the shade of the barn, shed, or trees, and panted due to the heat and weight of their thick coats.

The process of shearing in those early days required two or three pairs of scissors and as many experienced persons to shear. A board about the size of a door was laid directly on the barn floor or sometimes raised on supports to allow for less back-bending work. A sheep was roped and guided to this platform. Then she was laid on her side, the two lower hooves bound, and the wool cutting began. Shearing became easier if the scissors were held parallel and near to the animal's body, and progressed from her belly to her back and up her neck. Often the lanolin-filled scissors were dipped into a can of water to help make cutting easier.

When one side was complete, the other two feet were tied together and the sheep was rolled over to lie on the newly cut fleece with its upper feet now free until the shearing was finished. Upon being released, the sheep quickly got up, gave its body a shake, and frolicked off to graze in comfort.

Each fleece, laden with heavy lanolin and barnyard debris, was then rolled into a large ball and tied with twine. At the end of the shearing process, all the bundles of wool were stored in a corner of the granary and forgotten until spring work was completed and perchance a nice rain filled the rain barrels. Wool was always washed by hand in the soft water, resulting in a white soft fluff that gave off a mild and pleasant aroma of lanolin. However, before that could be achieved, it was necessary to wash and rinse the wool several times before spreading it out to dry. Then the dry wool was collected and stored under a bed upstairs, and again forgotten until the winter.

The wool resurfaced after crops and gardens were harvested and preparations for winter were complete. Then on long winter nights a large bundle of wool was brought down from the upstairs and distributed among several members of the family, who set their chairs in a semi-circle in the middle of the large room that served as kitchen, dining room, and living room. As the family chatted or listened to the battery-operated radio, each member pulled gently but firmly on bits of wool, working more intently on matted areas, and so creating mounds of soft loose fluff beside each chair.

A couple of home-crafted combs for wool, made by Father, were used to rake the wool so that the fibres ran in one direction. These special tools looked like wooden spatulas with about ten long spikes pushed through the wide part of each paddle. Because with warm spikes the wool combed more easily, Mother always sat next to the stove where she could rest the combs on the end of the stove to keep them warm. The combs were pulled against each other in opposite directions, arranging the fibres lengthwise. Then the wool was gently pulled from each comb,

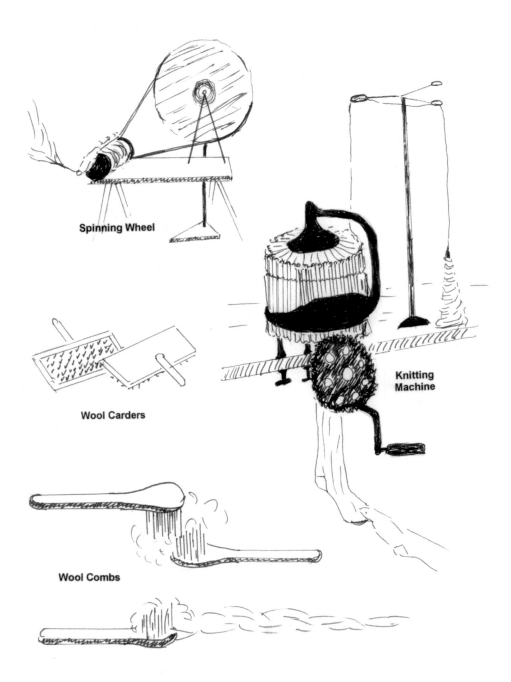

Spinning Wheel

Wool Carders

Knitting Machine

Wool Combs

Illustrated by Pearl Murray, 1995.

This wool carder made larger batts than small carders. Photo, 2003.

resulting in a metre-long, horse-tail-shaped length of wool, and was laid gently over the back of a chair to await the next step of the wool process—spinning the wool into yarn.

Father studied a commercially built spinning wheel, then built one, but changed the design so that the wheel was larger and the machine did not require the fast pumping of the pedal. Mother spun at a more leisurely pace with the same results. A knitting machine was purchased, consisting of a cylindrical shape with numerous hooks around its perimeter. By removing some hooks she could alter the design of the knit—"purl one and knit three" for stockings, whereas only knit was preferred for mittens. With the crank of a handle a complete circle was quickly knit. Knitting with the machine became more complicated when the heels and toes were to be knitted. At that time to be interrupted meant possible errors in the size of the garment Mother was creating.

Often at five o'clock on winter mornings, while the family slept soundly upstairs under wool quilts, the whir of the knitting machine downstairs accompanied

Shepherds Mike and Dan, 1927.

our dreams as socks, stockings, mittens, and tubes of knitting, to be used to make sweaters, were churned out.

Since telephones did not exist in the community at that time, neighbours often arrived unannounced with bulging bags which at one time had held sugar in them but now contained balls of their own homespun yarn for my mother to convert into garments the quick way. Mother charged about twenty-five cents to make a pair of socks. The money was minimal but with my mother's careful managing, her meagre earnings went a long way.

A residue of poor-quality wool was left on the combs by the process discussed earlier. That wool was also used. It was carded into squares of wool and eventually encased between two layers of cotton to make quilts. One would think that that was as far as the use of wool went. But no, Mother did more. Wool was too precious to throw in the garbage. Wool garments that developed holes, such as socks, were darned with new wool. However, if the holes became too large to darn, the garment was unravelled, resulting in bags full of various lengths of yarn. Again the family was called, to help tie the ends of yarn together and roll them into balls of knotted yarn. When enough of that yarn was collected, a wooden crochet hook that Father carved out of wood was used to make coverlets by combining three or four strands of the knotted yarn and crocheted as one heavy single strand. The knotted yarn gave the coverlet a rather artistic look. As well, when the cotton on the wool quilts became worn and tattered, the quilt was taken apart, the wool washed again, and then carded once more to be encased in a new set of cotton covers for a new quilt.

Wool is an almost indestructible fabric. It is very forgiving. Today, wool garments are expensive and often purchased by the elite, the folk who look for quality in garments. During our life on the homestead, we appreciated our woollen clothes but did not realize how fortunate we were to have our own abundant supply of such a marvellous natural fibre.

Chapter 17 A Massacre

During the long winter at the farm, our family's routine crystallized as solid as the frozen slough at the base of the sheep enclosure. Winter days were short, but not for a homesteader. Our days began in darkness and ended in darkness. Father and the boys worked outdoors. There were animals to feed, wood to chop, and harnesses to repair. Mother and her girls ran the household. There were cows to milk, clothes to wash and mend, little ones to care for, and bigger ones to be sent off to school.

But most especially there was wool—wool to be pulled to loosen fibres, wool to be carded, and wool to be spun into yarn. Wool was very important for our winter survival. Our socks were wool. Our hats were wool. We wore wool sweaters during the day and slept under wool quilts at night.

Bits of world news reached us over the crystal radio, but the world seemed far away from our frozen landscape. Our simple routine ran undisturbed, smoothly and peacefully. All was well with our world. But then, one memorable winter morning, the pendulum swung sharply from tranquillity and peace to chaos and anxiety. The family faced a sudden and abrupt upheaval.

That morning I was just finishing my porridge by the light of an oil lamp when Father walked in from the dark outdoors. It was usual for him to rise long before breakfast and feed the animals. But that morning something was different. He looked extremely distraught. His gaze focused on Mother, who was always the one who brought peace and quiet to desperate situations.

"Oh my God!" he groaned. "The sheep! The poor sheep!" As if searching for an answer to a question she knew nothing about, he looked at Mother. After a moment of startled silence he whispered, "At least one is dead. Some are injured. They were attacked during the night." He supported his head with an open palm.

"What do you mean?" Mother inquired anxiously.

"It's awful! Just awful!" He lowered his tall frame onto a chair near the door, gazed at the floor, and just continued to shake his head.

A low window in the gable of the upstairs presented a panoramic view of the whole south section of the farm. Through that window, in the summer, what first caught my eye was the water glistening in the sun. Ducks and geese swam or flapped their wings on the shore. But in winter the large flat expanse slept silently under rolling white blankets of snow. On this gentle slope between the house and the lake, the sheep enjoyed the warm southern exposure.

Father's disturbing report brought to mind an image of the previous evening. Before I climbed into bed, the landscape out the window presented a moonlit winter night with countless stars complementing the diamonds that sparkled on the snow. As they slept, the sheep looked like plump pillows tossed helter-skelter over a crumpled sheet of trampled snow. Content and happy, I crawled under the warm quilt.

That morning as we were about to leave for school, Father faced us. I thought he looked sad.

"I don't want this mentioned at school. It is important that we keep it quiet." As we left, I glanced towards the sheepfold where several animals struggled on the snow while the rest didn't sleep as they usually did this time of morning. They appeared frightened and stamped the snow with front feet as we approached the fence. We turned off to school, agreeing to follow Dad's orders.

The sun had almost set when we returned from school that afternoon—a warm, chinook day. A last carcass hung from a makeshift scaffold. Badly injured animals had been shorn, slaughtered, skinned, and the meat stored in the dugout freezer. We'd eat a lot of mutton this winter!

The animals found dead were not used for food; only the maimed were butchered. All the dead sheep had their wool removed. Our parents looked exhausted.

That evening, our parents and older brothers speculated as to the probable perpetrators of the massacre. I listened intently. It was unlikely that wolves, never seen in the area, or coyotes, often seen but not known to attack large animals, might have hurt our flock. It was concluded that the most likely attackers were dogs. They discussed the nature of the dogs in the neighbourhood. Could it have been our dog? Could our dog have joined forces with other dogs? No barking had been heard. Should father notify the RCMP? Could he be compensated for his losses? Not likely.

"Harry's dog follows him everywhere," Mike offered.

"Yeah! But would he leave their yard if Harry was not with him?" Dan laughed. Then he questioned: "What makes you think that coyotes weren't to blame?"

"Nah! Coyotes might steal a chicken but not attack a sheep."

"What about Petru's dog? He's big and scruffy and seems to be everywhere but at his home. Last week on my way to the post office I saw him wandering on the field near the corner. What was he doing there? He's powerful and I'd hate to be alone with him." I shivered.

"Nah! He lives way too far away to come here. Besides, how would he know we have sheep anyway? No, not him."

Would Father be compensated if it were a neighbour's dogs? Most home-steaders, during the economic recession, did not have two pennies to rub together. Several dry summers had yielded poor crops. That was the period referred to as "the dirty thirties."

Since few neighbours raised sheep, our animals would have been a curiosity to most dogs. It was likely that after the dogs got into the enclosure, they chased the animals around mostly for sport, and in their haste to escape, some sheep suffered injuries by slipping on an icy mound near the water trough.

"Oh, I fear they did enjoy the fun and will be back," Father added. "I'll keep our dog locked in the barn at night."

Father was obviously concerned. He often sat on the couch, rested his elbows on his knees, and gazed into space. He was easily annoyed with our noise and horseplay. He needed quiet time to think and plan.

Father began by enclosing our own dog in the barn every night. He listened for unusual sounds, even though he knew that sheep are silent when attacked. My dad occasionally got out of bed to glance out the gable window. In time, life at the homestead returned to its usual routine.

Was it instinct? Was it a yelp? Or did Mother, in fitful sleep, roll to his side of the bed? Father was up like a shot. He sensed something wrong and quickly glanced out the window. He bounded down the stairs and out the door in bare feet. He hollered loud enough to waken the dead! In the darkness he thought he saw a large animal jump the fence and disappear into the dark woods. As predicted, it had happened again, and the following day another animal had to be slaughtered.

This second attack was a fair indication that the intruder would be back. Sheep, when attacked, do not cry out like most animals, but they stamp a front hoof, hoping to scare off the intruder. And the sheep, comfortable in their woollen coats, prefer to sleep outdoors on straw rather than in the barn. Dad knew this and became more vigilant.

Would the attacks ever end? Would we get a peaceful night's sleep again?

The whole family routine tightened up. Everyone became vigilant. When I looked out the window at bedtime, I looked for attackers of sheep.

Father's routine changed too. Before retiring for the night, he spent a long time in the dark outdoors. When he returned, he looked tired and anxious. Often we were in bed before he got back.

Another dismal morning. It was a school day. We were having our porridge when Father walked in from the semi-darkness. He seemed to have a lifted spirit. He looked at Mother, nodded slightly, and in an almost inaudible whisper, he said, "I'll sleep well tonight."

Thereafter, the topic of the massacre was never discussed. Except for one major change: we complained that we had too many mutton dinners!

Weeks later our parents met Petru at the local post office. After exchanging comments about the weather, Petru remarked:

"My dog lost. He go and come and come and go and I tink dis time he get his self in lotta trouble."

"Oh, that's too bad," Father offered. Just then Mother touched his arm. "Let's go. It'll soon be dark."

"Yes," he agreed. And over his shoulder he called to Petru.

"Sorry about your dog. If I see him I'll let you know."

Chapter 18 A Price for Beauty

Seven sisters. Back row: Kathleen, Gladys, Helen and Pearl.
Front row: Adeline, Lucille and Bertha, 1940.

Even though farm girls during the Depression had few opportunities to acquire cosmetics, they took all measures available to them to help them look beautiful. They had no access to beauty products nor the money or opportunity to get them.

I recall my oldest sister wearing a wide-brimmed hat and long-sleeved shirt while working in the garden. Her goal was to avoid the sun's rays and so keep her "lily-white" complexion. Many city girls wore face powder, rouge, and lipstick. But more than liberal amounts of make-up had older people frowning and whispering behind their backs. My parents and most other parents did not allow their daughters to wear that "junk." They claimed that the girls were beautiful just as God had created them.

Smothered giggles from upstairs caught my attention, giggles by my three older sisters. What were they up to? I would try to find out. It was a lazy Sunday afternoon at the homestead. Sundays were days for rest; free days. I liked Sundays.

Dad napped on the cot in the summerhouse while Mother and I leisurely explored the garden. The boys were nowhere about. They had likely gone to the river where they would fish or just check the trash piles for treasures from Edmonton deposited by the water in a cove that was known for collecting junk. For a change, except for the occasional honk of a goose or a lamb's bleat, or the buzz of an insect, the farmyard was silent and free of human voices.

It was when I left the garden, trudged up the hill, and poked my nose into the big house that I heard the giggles.

Quietly I made my way up the long flight of narrow stairs and hid behind the whitewashed chimney which went through the second floor to the roof.

My three older sisters huddled on the floor. Gladys's secret shoebox, generally kept hidden under a bed, was in their midst. The girls giggled and whispered. What were they up to?

Because they bent over Kathleen, the youngest of the three, and concentrated on her face, they did not notice me approach. But when they saw me look down at them, they quickly covered their mouths with their hands. But it was too late. I saw red. My first reaction was that they were bleeding. They looked interesting. I wanted to be a part of it, so I knelt down beside them.

"I want that too," I begged.

"No. This is for big girls only. You are too small."

"But I'm almost as big as she," I added, pointing to Kathleen who was only a year older than I.

"Go away. You are too small for this. Go away right now and don't you dare tell Mom or Dad."

With lowered head I retraced my steps down the stairs. A feeling of sadness filled my soul. I felt unwanted, unloved, and alone. After all, Kathleen was only a year older than I. She was not a big girl. Why would they not share their secrets with me? And where did they get the red stuff to colour their mouths? I wished that I could get some too.

The sheep were busy mowing the grass around the house. Mother continued to check her garden, bending over now and then to pull a weed. I wandered towards the flower garden near the summerhouse. Even though the sheep were doing a thorough job, they avoided a variety of native plants that grew along the garden fence. That was too bad because one particular low plant looked beautiful. It had spiked branches with attractive leaves running up each spike. Along the spikes at regular intervals were little red berries. Red berries. Red! Red that could colour a mouth like my sisters'! I was glad that the sheep had not grazed the plants.

The red berries felt spongy in my little hand. The colour was a cool, faded red, not the warm colour that my sisters used. But it was red nevertheless. It would do.

One by one I smeared the berries on my mouth. Juice ran down my chin. It tasted awful. Was that why the sheep did not graze them? But I felt confident that I looked as pretty as my sisters. It did not occur to me to look in a mirror. I walked around the barnyard showing off to the poultry and grazing sheep. None seemed to notice.

I sat on the front steps and waited for Mother to come up from the garden. In the meantime my sisters came out the door. The red on their mouths was there no more except for a small trace on one side of Kathleen's mouth. I wondered what it was all about.

Helen noticed me first. She gasped. "What have you done to yourself? Your face is a mess."

I ran inside to look in the mirror. I was horrified. My face was a mess! I felt embarrassed and humiliated and anything but beautiful. I hoped that my sisters would not tell anyone. But then, I thought, if they did, I would tell on them.

Beauty comes at a price!

Chapter 19 The Tricky Turkey Hen

The turkey plunged into the woods. Pastel, 1970.

Mother looked out the summerhouse door.
"She's gone!" she exclaimed. "She's gone again. That bird is up to something and I aim to find out what."

He squirmed under the fence.

Steve squirmed under the barbed wire fence. Pastel, 1970.

A lone turkey appeared busy pecking at grasses and bugs near the house. She slowly drifted towards the gate. Minutes later, she vanished. Mother had observed similar behaviour at an earlier date. Why wasn't that turkey with the flock and where did she go?

"I have a feeling that she prefers her own choice of location for a nest. I set up several nests in the pen for the laying but she has a mind of her own. It is obvious that while she is near the house, she pretends everything is normal. But when no one is looking, she slips under the gate and into the bushes across the road."

Past experience taught Mother that turkeys are notorious for that type of behaviour. But having a nest in the woods might expose her to coyotes or other marauding animals. Mother wanted her nesting birds in a safe place.

Several days later, the lone hen seemed up to her old tricks again.

"Please keep an eye on that turkey. Remember the spot where she enters the woods. Then we may find her nest."

Mother's other family—her poultry, 1940.

Lucille (Dan's daughter) with Dan and George, dog and turkey, 1957.

Days later, the turkey appeared again. Family members glanced out the door from time to time. The turkey casually pecked her way towards the gate. And then, in an instant, she was gone! No one saw her disappear. It was as though she evaporated into thin air. The hen tricked everyone again.

Steve, who was ten years old, without sharing his plan, decided he would get even with the trickery. The next time the bird grazed in the yard, he lay silently and patiently in tall grasses along the fence. He waited and watched for what seemed like an eternity. The turkey slowly pecked her way towards the gate and then, like a flash, with head low, slipped under the gate and dashed towards the hazel nut bushes.

Slowly and silently, Steve followed. Only a short distance into the underbrush he spotted the bird crouched down in thick grasses. Once more, he waited patiently until she returned to the barnyard.

There were four speckled eggs in the crude nest.

His chest puffed up when he entered the summerhouse.

"I found it!" he announced proudly. "I found it! Four eggs." He could hardly control his emotions. "Right there. In the hazel bushes."

Mother, with Steve following closely and offering to help at every opportunity, provided the turkey hen with the eggs she had laid and new quarters where she could safely hatch her brood.

Chapter 20 The Squeaky Granary Door

Storage for grain and chop mill. Squeaky door on far end.
Oil, Bill Lorenz, 1970.

When a grain grinder, called a "chopper," was acquired for our homestead, it was installed in the north room at the end of the long log granary. Except for the horses, who were fed oats, most farm animals, and especially the young poultry, flourished when fed ground grain.

After many years of constant use, the door to the chop room became squeaky and it became more irritating as time went on. Mother asked her men to oil the hinges, but somehow it never got done. She found the squeak a nuisance because, as with Pavlov's dog, when the chickens, turkeys, and sheep heard the squeak they rushed to the granary to glean any grain spilled on the chop room floor.

If Mother did not close the door quickly, she suffered the brunt of the unruly animals. They rudely invaded the small chop room. The sheep were particularly obnoxious, but although they pushed against the small woman, she was not hurt. When thrown off balance, she landed on top of a soft and woolly back.

One summer day it was "bread day" again. Mother was busier than usual on bread days. She was up at the crack of dawn to begin the yeast batter. Later it was mixed into firm dough. A mental schedule was made, planning the kneading, shaping of loaves, and heating of the outdoor oven. Twenty loaves of bread would keep her large family fed for another week.

She glanced at the large basin that held the puffed-up batch of dough and calculated the time for a second punching down. She would have just enough time to get the cream into the butter churn and then get one of her children to crank the handle.

Just then, she heard a commotion outside the summerhouse. As she looked out the open door, she noticed her flock of more than twenty turkeys was extremely agitated. Excited gobbling noises drowned out the family's conversation. Then the turkeys ran and flew past the house, heading towards the gate and the road allowance. They paid no heed to the fence built to confine them to the barnyard area. They were attracted by the calls of turkeys foreign to Mother's flock.

Mother could not understand the cause for the bizarre behaviour so she ran out to check.

A neighbour ran over the brow of the hill towards our gate. There the noisy birds strutted and gobbled loudly. "My turkeys escaped," she called excitedly. "And they have joined your flock. Oh dear! Oh dear!"

After much discussion between the two women about how the birds might be identified and sorted, it seemed impossible to reach a solution. The turkeys moved constantly and greeted the new acquaintances in turkey fashion.

Oh dear, Mother thought. I don't need the extra pressure today. The bread should have been kneaded some time ago. The men want an early lunch before they leave for the hay field. The butter needs my attention. She looked at the birds.

"Well, I'll just take seven turkeys and leave," Mother heard the neighbour say. Some turkeys in the group were scrawny and small. Mother did not like the neighbour's suggestion about claiming just any seven turkeys. She wanted her own healthy birds. The stressful situation blurred her thinking. If only my husband were here, she thought, he would know what to do. Oh dear God, please help.

Just then in addition to the gobbling noise of the turkeys, a familiar, irritating, and embarrassing sound was heard from the barnyard. Dan, her son, had just opened the chop room door. The sound was familiar to Mother's flock of turkeys too. At that moment a large number of turkeys left the area near the gate and hurried towards the granary.

Six small birds remained near the gate. They seemed lost and confused, wondering why they were abandoned so abruptly. But they were not aware of the significance of the squeaky door.

That squeaky granary door saved Mother's day. Sorting the turkeys had been done quickly and effectively, and to her satisfaction.

Chapter 21 Memories of Deep Lake School

We take the shortcut across the field. Pastel, 1980.

We rose in the dark and made our way downstairs. By the light of the kerosene lamp we ate our porridge, made two sandwiches each with homemade jam, homemade cheese, or peanut butter—never meat. In the winter we walked along the road. To get to our school it took one hour to walk one and a half miles south and then the same distance west.

Warm, mostly woollen clothes kept us comfortable. We didn't know about fashion. For girls, wearing slacks was an unknown. Woollen stockings and mittens knitted by Mother on a knitting machine, fleece-lined bloomers, coats worn over skirts or dresses, toques and felt boots kept us warm. One family we walked with did not fare as well. A small boy often cried because his hands were cold. I put my mitts over his and then pushed the hand with which I carried my books into the coat front and the other in my pocket. Backpacks did not exist.

Often in the morning one of us couldn't find mittens or socks. It seemed that Mother was always the one who found them. She methodically went through all the clothes that had been thrown on a small cot near the stairs and came up with the lost article. I wonder how she cared for such a large family and remained so calm.

On our long trek to and from school we learned about nature. A flock of grouse or partridges took flight as we approached. Canada geese and cranes called from the skies and reminded us of the season. We welcomed them in the spring and said goodbye in the fall. A meadowlark greeted us with its song. Now and then we met rabbits, skunks, or porcupines, but usually just lots of gophers—or perhaps they should have been called Richardson ground squirrels—as we learned at school. We knew where lady's slippers and shooting stars grew and watched for their appearance. Mother was delighted when in the early spring, even before the garden was planted, we brought home morels or wild onions. She sautéd the mushrooms in sour cream. Mmm! Delicious! The onions she used in soups or chopped over mashed potatoes or meat.

In the spring and fall we walked across farms, like following a hypotenuse on a right-angled triangle. It reduced our walking distance by almost a mile. At the end of our farm we crossed the fence to the neighbour's farm, and then made our way through dense bushes, crossed a bog, and we were at another farm. When traversing fields of grain, we walked in single file to avoid trampling much grain. In the spring the grain shoots were short and green. When we returned in the fall, the tall grain was a golden brown. And then the stooks appeared.

On hot days when we returned from school, we stopped at the well at a farmyard to quench our thirst. We drew a pail of water from the well, tipped it, and drank right from the pail. We feared the farmer: a big, burly man with bushy eyebrows and a rather large nose. But one day he hung a metal cup on a nail on the well for our use. He was a kind man after all.

The school day ran from 9:00 a.m. to 4:00 p.m. with one hour for lunch and two fifteen-minute recesses; no playground supervision.

The school bell rang. We stood by our desks and recited the Lord's Prayer. As we faced the Union Jack that hung above the front blackboard, we sang "God Save the King."

The room was large, with an oiled floor, and furnished with rows of double desks. Little panes of glass covered the whole east side. The front and west walls were all blackboard. Our library, a cupboard in a corner, had glass doors and three shelves containing about fifty books. A stove shaped like an oil drum lay on top of supports. It occupied the centre area near the back. To prevent accidents, a thick aluminum shield surrounded it on three sides. In the winter large blocks of wood were stacked in the boys' cloakroom. We had no coal.

The teacher's desk at the front of the room contained two important items: the daily register and a strap. When we lined up behind the desk to take turns reading aloud from our readers, our teacher sometimes leaned his chair backwards and rested his feet on the top of the desk.

When I started school, there were 42 pupils attending. The senior pupils, grades seven and eight, sat in the row nearest the windows. First graders were on the dark opposite side.

We sat down. Two senior pupils were health inspectors for the week. They walked up and down the rows and checked each child for cleanliness and neatness. They checked hands and nails, ears, neck, hair, and handkerchiefs. Kleenex was still unknown. When it was my turn to be health inspector, I noticed a boy pull a neatly folded handkerchief from his shirt pocket. It has been folded and unfolded so many times that it resembled a checkerboard. It was obvious that its main purpose was for the inspection. When his nose dripped, he simply drew his arm across his face to wipe it with his shirtsleeve.

After health inspection, we reported current events.

Boys' and girls' outhouses were a fair distance from the school, one on either side of a knoll. Trips to the outhouse were brief when temperatures were extremely cold. During pleasant days, however, I preferred to take my time and sing rather than rush back to the classroom.

The first time I saw a flush toilet was when I was thirteen years old and went to the town school. At first I was not sure about its use or its operation. But there were no outhouses in the schoolyard in town.

At the beginning of the school year we were given textbooks for arithmetic, spelling, and reading. For the higher grades, the teacher had assignment pages written on the blackboard. He worked with the primary grades first and then moved up, with pupils marking the previous day's assignments. As needed, he introduced new concepts.

When I was in seventh grade he sometimes asked me to go to the blackboard near the back to help the three boys in my grade with math problems.

All core subjects were treated in this manner. However, classes were often combined for subjects like health, social studies, science, and music.

Our water supply came from a pump in the yard. On winter mornings a large pot was filled with water and set on the top of the stove. By noon it was hot. The school system provided us with cans of cocoa. Each family took turns bringing a quart jar of milk to add to the cocoa. Families that had more milk brought more, for a tastier hot drink. For variety, sometimes we exchanged a half sandwich with another pupil.

Most days I saved a half sandwich to eat on the way home from school to give me energy to walk the three miles. But one day after school my brown paper lunch bag was not on the cloakroom shelf where lunches were kept. It continued to disappear every now and then. Someone else was hungry too.

In the winter we played football or Fox and Goose. In summer it was softball, rounders, tag, or hide and seek. Neighbouring schools, Desjarlais, about five miles west, or Ispas, on the east, came to our school on some Friday afternoons to play softball. They arrived in the back of a farmer's truck or in a wagon. Our school took part in a junior high girls' softball tournament in the town of Willingdon. Because we were a country school, we were permitted to have up to three boys on our team but they could not play key positions. I was in fourth grade, when my brother Nick, in eighth grade, hit several home runs. Our pitcher, Elizabeth, performed with a mean and swift delivery. We won the game! Our opponents were embarrassed and angry. "Not fair," they complained.

A health team visited our school. Each child in turn got a scratch on the upper arm—smallpox vaccination. A small boy was frightened. He ran out and hid behind the school.

By the time I was in sixth grade, our library situation had improved. The school system established a travelling library. Every two or three months, a wooden box about the size of a small trunk, full of books, arrived from Desjarlais School. The box we had was sent on to Ispas. I was delighted with the new reading material.

Before the Christmas concert, boards and supports stored in the barn were brought to the school and a stage was erected. Sheets were used for curtains. We had no electricity so neighbours lent us gas lamps that were well pumped before the concert for good light all evening. Benches were borrowed from homes for extra seating. Christmas concerts were a must. We had one every year.

Several days after my studies at the Deep Lake School were over for good, our beloved school mysteriously burned down. Because over the years the pupil population had declined, a smaller building was quickly built. More modern materials were used. But sadly, it did not compare with the old school. I was glad that I didn't have to return.

In country school settings, pupils didn't get the one-on-one attention that one might expect in town schools where one teacher was responsible for only one grade, but because the teacher in a country school worked with many grades, pupils learned to work on their own. One had to admire teachers who were committed to country schools. Soon after the first day of school an understanding was established towards working independently.

Do I feel cheated to have been at a country school? Never!

Chapter 22 Mother Nature's Cruel Trick

Sporting activities, 1950.

To watch our future days of fun disappear before our eyes brought feelings of sorrow and hopelessness.

Even though the wind blew furiously, we went out for a lunchtime game of football played in Deep Lake School style. It was the only outdoor competitive sport available to us because the ball we used was the one and only piece of winter playground equipment requisitioned by our school board. As well, all pupils from grades one to eight could participate.

We took the big red ball for granted and had no extraordinary appreciation for it until one windy day in mid-winter.

Two thick branches embedded in the snow at each end of the playing field were the goal posts. In our style of football, fancy footwork was important to move the ball towards the opponents' goal. Use of hands was not allowed. Occasionally we played another version of the game in which both hands and feet were used. But most often the no-hands game was the popular one.

On that particular windy day, extra skills were needed. After a gentle kick, the light ball, whipped along by the strong wind, often stopped in the caragana shrubs and maple trees that surrounded the school grounds. However, during one such kick, the wind guided the ball down a gentle slope towards the only opening in the shrubs, the open gate to the schoolyard.

One of the boys ran to retrieve it, only to see it go steadily through the opening, defiantly cross the road, and continue into an open field covered with much snow.

"Oh no!" he called in dismay. "It's gone! It's gone!"

We ran out the gate and watched the ball move steadily on top of the snow. It grew smaller and smaller as it rolled merrily north across the white, rolling expanse. It moved up one rise and then disappeared. Moments later a smaller speck climbed a second rise.

"It won't go up that big hill," one of the boys offered. Most of us silently clasped our hands to our chests hoping the ball would stop. Then a tiny speck that could hardly be seen slowly progressed up the last big hill. It faltered, rolled back, and then tried again. Although some children were convinced that it went over the top, others thought it had rolled back into the hidden valley. It was too far away to be certain.

"If it went over that last hill it will be on its way to the river. We will not see it again until the snow melts. I think it will stop in the ravine by the river. We may find it in the summer."

Many agreed with that possibility. But what do we do in the meantime? How do we survive without a football? Fox and Goose was a popular game but it could be played only after a snowfall when the pie-shaped design could be drawn in the fresh snow. Sledding was fun too, but boring after the first few runs. Football was our most popular sport.

If the teacher asked the school board for another ball, it could take months to get it. The board was reluctant to let schools have equipment even though that was its intended purpose. They questioned every detail, took weeks to consider it, and in the end sent it out at their own discretion.

To try to retrieve the ball even if it did not go over the last hill was out of the question. We realized that it would be difficult and likely impossible for a child to trudge through waist-deep snow for half a mile.

The whole student body of more than thirty stood on the road and faced north with the wind pushing at our backs. In the distance the blue sky became blue-grey as it neared the horizon, then darkened at the hills and trees beyond the river. The last rise was a bright white contrast against the dark background. We stared in silence.

The football returns. Pastels, 2009.

Eventually the silence was broken. "I . . . I . . . I'd like to try it," my brother Steve, age twelve, whispered hesitantly. The group broke its silence and the arguments were all negative.

"Don't do it."

"The snow is far too deep."

"You'll get buried alive in all that snow."

Where the weeds grew along the edge of the field, Steve floundered through deep snow. It was a disappointing start. However, after the first hurdle, he discovered that the surface of the wind-whipped snow was a hard crust that supported him. With small shuffling baby steps he moved forward. It would take a long time.

We watched him progress on the surface until he reached the first low spot. There he sank, thrashed, and kicked and then climbed to the hard surface again. After the second hill, the top of his head was seen bobbing up and down. He was progressing well. Then he disappeared completely in the valley in front of the last high hill.

The school bell rang but only the little ones ran inside. Although I was little too, I could not abandon my brother. I stayed.

Our teacher came out of the school. He pushed up his collar and wound his coat tightly around him as the wind tried to blow him away.

"What's going on?" he demanded. Responses were many.

"Our ball is gone."

"Steve is lost."

"We have no football."

"The wind blew it out the gate."

"It just kept rolling on and on."

"We can't see Steve."

Our teacher looked concerned. Would he have to look for the lost child? He wondered aloud if the crusted snow would support his weight. Where was Steve? Was he safe?

My brother had disappeared. Could he see the ball or was it gone forever? But where was he? Was he buried alive in the deep snow?

Eventually a speck emerged in the distance. Slowly, very slowly it grew larger. Now feeling very cold from the wind's relentless beating, we huddled more closely, all eyes focused ahead.

After what seemed like an eternity, Steve drew nearer. He bent forward to avoid the biting wind on his face.

Under his arm was a red ball.

A sure sign of spring. Watercolour, 1980.

Pearl's calla lilies. Watercolour, 1980.

Spring at the Farm

Days grow balmy
Rivulets flow
The sky is brighter
The grasses grow

Dandelions awaken
Cover the ground
Morels and leeks
Can also be found
With food from the earth
The family enjoys
And eat it with mirth

Spring emerges
It kills the snow
It brings new life
And soft breezes blow

Chapter 23 The Christmas Tree

Christmas was coming to Deep Lake School once again, and with it, the yearly school Christmas concert. At the school the stage had been assembled, the bed-sheet curtains hung, and the sound of rehearsals filled the afternoon air. And with only three days left before the performance it was time to fetch the school Christmas tree from the banks of the nearby North Saskatchewan River.

As he did every year, our teacher put three boys in charge of getting the tree. They would have to walk almost a mile to the river, find a suitable spruce, chop it down, and drag it back to the school. The job required responsibility and size, and our teacher selected only boys from the eighth grade, the biggest boys in the school. My brother Steve was one of the lucky three.

Off they went, axe over shoulder, while the rest of us remained at school.

That afternoon passed quickly with rehearsals, singing, and so on. The early winter sunset turned the outside to night. School was over, we were dismissed, and still the eighth grade boys had not returned with the tree. The teacher looked concerned. Just as we were about to leave, the boys appeared dragging a spruce tree. When our teacher asked them what took so long, the boys looked down at their feet and muttered incoherently. With a few stern words on the evils of dawdling, the teacher sent them on their way.

On the way home, Steve was not his usual boisterous self. He walked in silence, his head hung low.

"What took you so long?" I asked. "The teacher was worried."

Steve looked up. His eyes filled with tears and then he blurted out, "I'm in big trouble."

"But why? What happened?" Steve stood in the snow, his face writhing as he fought with his emotions. But slowly, in fits and starts, the story came out. He finished by saying in a quavering voice, "What will happen if the RCMP come to our house? Dad will kill me!" He turned and bolted down the road towards our farm.

The rest of us followed more slowly, turning the matter over between us. We knew that Father would be furious when he found out. We knew the right thing to do would be to tell him, but how to do it? Who had the guts? Father was strict. He

In winter, all spruce are Christmas trees at night.
Watercolour, 1997.

believed in staying out of trouble at all costs. We knew his interrogation, delivered in that stern voice from his great height, with lowering eyebrows and piercing eyes, would reduce Steve to *pulp*—it would do the same to any of us. And when Dad heard that the police were coming to our house . . . well, none of us would want to be there when that happened.

I recalled an earlier incident when my brother Nick broke a window at school. It happened after recess when the teacher rang the bell. As Nick ran, he kicked a football, which sailed through the school window. Nick owed the teacher twenty-five cents for the replacement pane. But Nick had no money, and neither did any of us. He did not dare tell Father.

Every day, the teacher asked for the money. Each time Nick squirmed in his desk and uttered a lame excuse.

Nick wanted to tell Father, but was afraid. In cases like those, Dad was determined to know all facts—what, how, where, and especially why. We avoided Dad's interrogations at any cost.

One evening, however, Nick grabbed my eraser and would not return it.

"Give it back," I demanded, "or I'll tell about the window."

Immediately a loud voice questioned, "What window?" The secret was out and Dad put Nick through the *third degree*. In the end, Nick was given twenty-five cents to pay for the window.

But today's situation was even more serious—the police were involved!

That evening wore on, each of us dreading the knock at the door when the Mounties came to tell Father. It was hardest on Steve. I cornered him upstairs in our communal bedroom.

"Steve," I whispered, "You've got to tell Father."

"I can't! I can't!" he hissed back. "Maybe the Mounties won't come, maybe Father won't find out."

There was a heavy footfall on the top of the stairs. We froze. "Find out what!" came Father's voice from the gloom. Steve paled. While looking down at the floor, he told his story, fearfully sharing the events of the afternoon and unburdening his heavy heart.

The boys had walked to the river for a Christmas tree. They reached the valley where spruce spread their fragrant branches all around them.

They cut one down. But before they left, they noticed smoke rising several hundred feet from where they stood.

"See that smoke? I wonder what is burning here in the forest," one of the boys offered.

"Let's go see." They decided to investigate and then pick up the tree on their way back.

The source of the smoke was concealed by spruce trees and bushes. When they made their way around the brushy screen, they gazed in amazement.

They saw pipes and utensils. They heard bubbling sounds and were aware of a sweet aroma. They warmed their hands over dying embers. A sled nearby held a box with two jugs in it. They removed the box and slid down the slope. After several trips, one of the runners collapsed. They returned to the strange mass of pipes. One of the boys touched a pipe, causing the setup to collapse. They tried to set it right but it only became worse.

As they concentrated on fixing the pipes, they heard a dog bark, crunching footsteps in the snow, and a man yelling angrily. The man rushed towards them, yelling, swearing, and waving a stick. Then he threatened to notify the police. He told them that they would surely go to jail. The boys ran. They grabbed the tree and hurried back to the school.

As Steve gave his account of what happened that afternoon, Father remained amazingly silent. Curiously, Steve cast a glance up to Father's face. He expected to see anger but instead he saw a curious smile on his father's face. Then, Father slapped his knee and broke out in laughter. Steve was so surprised he almost fell from his chair.

"It was wrong of you to touch another person's property," Father pointed out, "but the police will not come for you."

The still was hidden in the valley because it was illegal to make home brew. By reporting the boys, the man would only incriminate himself.

That evening we added a new word to our vocabulary: "Moonshine."

Chapter 24 A Hidden Treasure

Mother was delighted to feed the wild grey goose that wintered with her flock. 1970.

We heard the honking of geese from the barnyard. Mother looked out the window.

"It is time. But please be careful," she cautioned as she handed me a small bucket. It was lined with a soft old towel, crumpled on the bottom of the pail and pulled partly up its sides.

"Do you want to come with me, Lucy? We'll look for a surprise." Lucy was four years old, with a chubby, round face and dark eyes that peered out from behind a mass of curly brown hair.

"Yes! Yes!" she responded excitedly and then ran to fetch her sweater.

At the age of nine, I still wondered how my mother knew it was time. However, as I grew older, by watching and listening over the years, I too learned the language of geese.

I learned to tell when they were happy. For example, on warm summer days after a luxurious swim on the nearby pond, the flock performed a series of quick, short honks, accompanied by the sound of flapping wings. Following that was more intense honking, and a sudden shallow flight. Wing tips and webbed feet skimmed the ground as the geese flew, and then landed near the granary. There, the honks became muffled as the geese searched for the wheat and oat seeds they had missed during the morning feeding. This was their way of saying that all was well in the world.

Fewer honks with much hissing indicated an intruder had invaded their territory, such as a dog, a lamb, or a curious nine-year-old girl who had come too near. Their bent necks and bobbing heads made snake-like movements. A nip on the leg sent the intruder fleeing, and resulted in a loud chorus of hurrahs, with heads held high and much discussion of the battle. They praised one another for the victory.

But this morning's goose language implied a different situation and my mother understood it. A torrent of high-sounding honks emanated from one goose as she left the pen and waddled into the bright sunlight. She seemed to be making a happy announcement. "I did it!" she was saying, "I have delivered! I will have a family!"

As she advanced towards the rest of the flock, they rushed to meet her, responding in low-pitched honks, their heads bobbing in front of the special goose.

"Congratulations! You did well! We'll look forward to welcoming your little one to the flock!"

Lucy and I walked down the slope towards the shed where the geese lived, Lucy's little hand holding tightly to the handle of the bucket.

In summer, the flock of geese numbered about two dozen, but only three breeding females and one gander were kept throughout the winter. The geese were not happy at our approach. Long weaving necks and continuous hissing sounds warned us to move with caution. We sidled along the outer wall of the shed, then ducked into the low open door, pulling it shut behind us. Enough light came through the small dirty window to illuminate the shapes of three crude nests, located in the corners of the little room.

"Where is the egg, Lucy?" I whispered to my sister, eager to make the most of her new experience.

"I dunno. I can't see no egg."

"The goose covers it with straw, so no one sees it. And to keep it warm."

We examined a nest that had its hollow filled with bits of straw and soft down. Lucy timidly pushed her plump hands under the mound of fluff.

"It's here! It's warm." She squealed excitedly, "I'll put it in the pail." Holding it with both of her little hands, she lowered the large egg gently into the bucket. As we made our way back up the sandy incline towards the house, Lucy skipped happily.

For about two weeks, the eggs would be collected regularly until the goose showed signs of "clucking." Clucking meant she would remain on the nest. The nest would then be filled with the collected eggs. After three weeks of sitting on her eggs and keeping them warm, a gaggle of fuzzy goslings would hatch and follow mother goose down to the pond.

To hold a warm fluffy baby goose in the palm of one's hand and feel its curious pecks on your fingers, lips, and cheeks is a sensation that you never forget. Goslings are miracles of God. They are treasures to love.

Mother's geese. Sketch, 1985.

Chapter 25 Goodbye Frank—Hello Roan

George, Steve, Nick, Dan, Mike with horses, 1935.

Our family looked forward to the annual Hairy Hill "picnic" in July. We left the homestead, the chores, and daily routine, to spend the day having fun. It was regarded as our holiday—our vacation.

This was the day, but the car could not accommodate our large family. We numbered fifteen in all: two adults and thirteen children. Father, Mother, and the four youngest would ride in the car. One or two unlucky ones would look after the farm. The rest of us, including me, would travel by horses and buggy. It was twelve miles to Hairy Hill, so the buggy was given a head start. Two older brothers would be in charge of the driving and care of the horses once we arrived in town. Last-minute instructions were given and we climbed into the buggy.

"Drive sensibly."

"If you get to town before us, make sure you water the horses at the town trough and give them some hay."

"Go directly to the school grounds." Instructions became less clear as we left through the open gate.

We had travelled only a few miles, when Frank, the most handsome of our four horses, started behaving strangely. His step faltered. He often turned his head to look backwards. I thought he looked sad. Nick pulled the buggy off the road onto a grassy area. Brown grazed eagerly, lips stretching as far as they would go, while Frank lay on the ground, harness and all. He continued to look towards his stomach. Something was very wrong and it frightened us. What should we do? We waited anxiously.

Our car, followed by clouds of dust, was a welcome sight. Our parents were coming. They would know what to do.

Father examined the horse. Frank was obviously ill. Father's grave expression was anything but encouraging. Frank was urged to stand. It was decided that two of my older brothers would guide the team homeward at a slow pace, while the rest of us squeezed into the 1927 Essex and continued on to Hairy Hill.

Our day of fun was short-lived because Father was eager to get back to the farm to check his sick animal. His horses were important for our livelihood.

That evening, as we ate our dinner, the conversation changed from the picnic to Frank. My dad sadly shook his head.

"He's a very sick horse. I doubt he will pull through."

The following day Frank lay listless in the pasture near our barn. He hardly tasted the water we offered him. Father came by often, looking concerned. He decided against calling the neighbour who treated sick animals by "blood-letting." No, Dad was convinced that the bloated stomach indicated a digestive problem.

Frank was our only dapple-grey. He had been a strong and gentle animal. I feared him only one time — but the fault was mine.

It happened one sunny day when Frank grazed in a meadow. I approached him and stroked his smooth back. Nasty horseflies flew about his front legs, darting in and out as they laid their eggs on the coarse fetlocks. I remembered Father saying that when horses rubbed their itchy fetlocks, the eggs transferred to the animal's mouth. Dad's theory was that the eggs were harboured under the upper lip, hatched, and were eventually ingested — thus beginning the reproductive cycle.

To reduce the number of horseflies buzzing around Frank's feet, I followed the grazing horse, swatting at the flies. He was annoyed. He wished to graze in peace. Finally, with ears bent back and teeth bared, he lunged towards me, but did not bite. I took the hint and left quickly.

Now, as Frank lay on the ground, Father stopped by. My sister and I gently brushed Frank's back and stroked his face. Dad looked down sadly at the three of us.

View of team from the top of a load of hay. Sketch, 1985.

"I'm sorry that you are so sick," I cried to Frank, as tears filled my eyes.

The following morning when I awoke, I looked out the upstairs window towards the barnyard where I had hugged Frank and bid him good night. Frank was not there.

"Frank is all better," I called, as I clasped my hands in hope.

Then I spotted Father walking behind a harnessed team dragging a double-tree (this was the bar behind the horses that normally connected them to an implement or load, but in this case the load was missing). They approached the barn from the pasture beyond which lay a deep, wooded ravine. Mother went out to meet Dad and I followed her.

"There were worms in his stomach—both in and outside the intestines. Those dreadful horseflies. Nothing would have saved him, not medicine, not 'blood-letting.' Poor Frank! He didn't have a chance," mourned my father.

Then I understood. Father had pulled the horse's body to the ravine, our *animal cemetery*.

Harvest time approached quickly. The green fields miraculously turned golden. Father was anxious. Four horses were needed to pull the binder, and then haul the sheaves to the thresher. He needed a horse, but horses were not readily available.

In desperation, Father asked a neighbour if he had an extra horse. At first the man was non-committal. Then he reluctantly admitted he did have an animal he seldom used, because it was so wild. He might consider selling it, but did not think Dad would be interested. He certainly did not wish to bring the horse to the barn.

But Father was insistent. He was determined he could train a wild horse, even though the time was short.

After much discussion, the men brought the horses into a corral. The neighbour pointed to a roan of smaller stature than Frank. The horse shook and shied when his master came near—a peculiar behaviour. Then Father noticed a strange stripe across the horse's back. Tufts of white hair grew along its length.

Aha, thought Father. This horse had been abused. It's been beaten—beaten badly enough to break the skin. He concluded the horse was wild because it was afraid and did not trust people. Dad bought it for $35.

Because we referred to the new horse as "the roan" we eventually adopted that name. At first Roan displayed impossible behaviour when anyone approached. He nervously shied away and snorted. It was important to win his confidence.

Dad advised us to make our presence obvious whenever we entered the barn—we should whistle or talk in gentle tones. An unexpected move near Roan sent him quivering and pulling on the rope.

Gradually, with gentle talk, a special measure of oats, and a slow and gentle touch, the frightened horse began to trust us. Although we were never able to ride Roan, he worked well beside the other horses and that was good enough for my dad.

I cherish the memories of our horses and the part they played in my childhood. Frank and Roan helped me learn about life and death, patience and acceptance, trust and mistrust. Through them, I experienced the emotions of hate, fear, and anger, as well as sadness, hope, and love—love being the strongest of them all.

Chapter 26 Farmer Fred and Dentistry

Fred—master of his home, 1957.

During the Depression many a throbbing toothache was tolerated in resigned silence. With no local dentist and little or no money, the homesteaders at Deep Lake had limited choices. Although home remedies were constantly concocted, few were effective. Toothaches were a stubborn lot.

One hot day in July, my father was mowing hay on the far south meadow. He could see the house from his place of work. When the sun erased the shade on the west wall, it was time for him and the team to return home for food and rest.

Although he knew it was still mid-morning, he glanced towards the house out of habit. The west wall was still in shadow. However, Dad noticed a figure in the field, between him and the house. He did not recognize the person as one of his family. The short, round shape suggested that it might be George, a distant neighbour.

"Good morning, Fred, and God help you with your work."

"Good morning. That was a long walk. You could have driven here with your team."

"Oh no. Gates to open and close."

Dad noticed a piece of shiny metal protruding from a clasped hand. He was curious.

"What's new in the world today?" Dad asked, hoping to get some insight into the unusual visit. George did not waste Dad's precious time with small talk. He got right to the heart of matter.

"Fred, I need your help. I know that you are the only one around here who can help me."

Dad noticed that his neighbour looked poorly. But what was the matter and what did he conceal in his hand?

"I'm desperate, Fred. I'm in terrible pain. Three nights I haven't slept. This toothache is driving me crazy." He lowered his voice. "Fred, I want you to pull it out." He held out the pliers in his hand.

"George, George." Dad chuckled nervously. "You're not serious." But he knew that the man meant what he said. "I'm no dentist," he continued. "I can't do it. I'm sorry, but I won't do it."

"You must, Fred. I can't go on like this. I beg you to help me. There are five farms between your farm and mine. I didn't stop at any of them because I knew that only you might help me." Dad shook his head in disbelief.

After being subjected to relentless begging, he realized that George would not take no for an answer. Dad had to agree, much as he disliked the idea.

Before he could weaken and change his mind, Dad, tall and lanky, quickly wiped his sweaty palms on the back of his long trousers. He removed his hat and tossed it to the ground. Then he ran his arm across his brow and face, wiping the perspiration with his shirtsleeve. Again he wiped his hands, this time on the front of his shirt, which was cleaner than the grease-stained pants. He sat on the low wheel of the mower and spread wide his knees. George knelt in front of him. As in a vice, Dad held the patient between his knees. George pointed out the offending tooth, then reached into a pocket and withdrew a small flask of whisky. He took a slurp, then another which he held momentarily in his mouth, swished around, and spat on the ground.

"You'd better have some too," he offered.

"No, no. Not today."

With the big and awkward pliers, Dad clasped the molar. His knees tightened around George. Then, with determination, he clamped the tooth more firmly and pulled. At that moment George pulled away with a jerk and bellowed like a bull. Moaning and groaning, he covered his jaw with his hands and rolled on the ground.

But the tooth had not come out!

George had endured enough for one day. He resolved to suffer in silence until he could save enough money to see a dentist. Dad, too, was convinced that dentistry was not his profession. He would not try it again.

Several days later George again visited Dad.

"It's a miracle! Fred . . . Fred. My good friend Fred." My dad looked surprised. "Since you pulled my tooth, or tried to pull it, I haven't had a toothache. Not one! What a relief! And still I have my tooth. God bless you, my friend. God bless you. I will recommend you as the Deep Lake dentist."

Chapter 27 Our Moses Was a Girl

Maria with granddaughter Charlene Murray, 1960.

By 1930 the settlers in the Deep Lake district, situated about one hundred miles northeast of Edmonton, had completed the land improvements required to warrant ownership of their homesteads. Two schools had been built, as well as a small church for the Ukrainian Greek Orthodox residents of the community. Our family seldom attended the church because we did not know the Ukrainian language. So we welcomed the English-speaking missionaries who held Sunday School in our local school. Happily we learned about the Bible. While still very young, I mostly liked the stories of Noah's Ark, of Joseph and his multi-coloured coat, of David and Goliath, of the birth of Jesus, and the story of Baby Moses.

It was springtime again, my favourite time of year—a time of new beginnings. The barnyard was alive with baby animals. When Father came in for breakfast and announced the arrival of a new calf or lamb, I silently slipped out of the summerhouse and raced to the barn to welcome the newcomer. I did not question its origin. It was there. It filled my heart with joy. It was my new friend.

That too was the time of year when baby chicks, turkeys, and goslings emerged from eggshells. Although they entered the world looking wet and scrawny, minutes later they were miraculously transformed into lovable balls of down.

One day my older brother reported that the sow was having piglets. I hurried to the pigpen, found a crack between the logs and observed a larger than life pig, lying on her side. Her huge stomach hugged the ground. Two rows of buttons ran down her belly and clean, pink piglets already claimed their spots at the feeding stations. Turned-up snouts searched for food. They nuzzled the buttons, grabbed hold and held fast. A couple of little ones struggled to climb over their mother's extended hind legs. I thought they were smart little pigs, knowing how to curl their tiny tails so early in life. But I did not question where they came from. They were there. They were cute, and I loved them.

The month of June arrived. With the help of older family members, the garden was planted. The half-acre of potatoes, which would feed our large family during the winter, would soon begin to sprout. We collected dry fallen trees and dead branches from the roadsides for use in the outdoor oven. The firewood that was already cut, split, and stacked would be saved for winter.

I was too young to notice Mother's slow step, or the extra load she carried under a denim tent dress. Nor was I aware of the preparations being made for a special event, a time when Mother would be absent from her household duties.

In the summer, Mother could bake nearly twenty loaves of bread at a time in the outdoor oven. One memorable day my older sister punched down the large vat of dough, even though Mother generally preferred to do it herself. By late afternoon, a fire was lit in the clay oven. Eventually the aroma of fresh bread drifted throughout the yard. It made our mouths water.

Fred with grandson Douglas Murray, 1962.

Mother put a fresh loaf into a paper bag. She gave it to my brother Steve and asked him to take it down the hill to a neighbour who lived alone near the river.

"You go with him," she said as she looked at me.

We complained that we would feel awkward because the neighbour did not speak English. Mother put her hands on our shoulders, turned us towards the gate, and pushed gently.

"Hurry. Hurry," she pleaded. Something in her voice urged us to obey. Reluctantly we started off.

"Please hurry," she called again.

Rather than follow the big curve in the road, we ran straight down the fence line. In the low-lying area below, the river ran swiftly, making a swishing sound. Birds flitted about in the twilight and an owl hooted as we made our way downward.

Our pace slackened as we approached a log house, hardly visible in dark woods—only a few hundred yards from the south bank of the North Saskatchewan River.

Timidly we knocked on the door. A lady invited us in. She lived alone. Her husband had died and her only daughter, now a young lady, had left the farm to explore the big city of Edmonton. She was about to light a kerosene lamp, but instead opened the bag we offered her and smelled the fresh bread.

"Hmm," she muttered. Immediately, three slices were cut and then smeared with sour cream and shared. She took a large bite from her portion, all the while talking to us in a language we did not understand. Her hand motions indicated that we should leave.

We left quickly, but soon slowed our pace to finish the bread. Once done, we ran to the bottom of the curved road, which snaked up the steep hill to the top of the river valley. Steve grabbed my hand.

"Let's go straight up. It will be faster."

We pushed our way through the bush along the fence line, and climbed straight up the slope. We stopped to rest half-way up, where we checked a survey stake. Dad told us once that to tamper with it would be a criminal offence. Steve tried to wiggle it, but it stood firm.

"Five horses can't get this out!" he concluded.

On our return, the family was at the table, having a late dinner. Of course, dinner included lots of fresh bread. After dinner, Father lit the kerosene lamp. Mother claimed she was tired and left the summerhouse for the big house—our winter home and sleeping quarters. My older sisters were left to look after the dishes and chores.

A short while later, when I left for bed, I thought I saw our neighbour, whom we had just called on a short while earlier, lurking in the darkness. What was she doing here? How did she get here so quickly? Did she come around the big curve or follow our steps straight up the hill? Her visit at this time of day was most unusual!

The following morning Mother was not in the summerhouse to make the porridge. The boys complained that it was thick and lumpy.

"You can make it tomorrow," my sister Helen retaliated. Although Mother's absence was odd, I did not ask about her. At that time I was unaware she would be upstairs, lying in the east bedroom of the big house for a whole week.

When Gladys took a bowl of food to Mother, I followed and peeked out from behind my sister. It felt wrong to see Mother lying in bed. She always ran the household. Beside her was a soft-looking bundle. I stood on my toes and saw a round pink face with eyes closed. We had a baby!

"Where did the baby come from?" I wondered. I would try to find out.

Sometime later I approached my older brother.

"Where did the baby come from?" I asked. Nick tried to change the subject. Births were not talked about in those days. Babies appeared, they were accepted and loved, and they just were there. I squeezed his arm and repeated my question. He looked in the distance and shifted his weight from one foot to the other.

I dug my little fingers into his arm. "Where? Where?" I persisted.

"Well. Well," he stammered. "Remember Sunday School last Sunday? Remember the story of Baby Moses on the river? Remember our neighbour was here last night?

"Well, she found the baby on the river—like Moses. She thought it would be happy with brothers and sisters, so she brought it to our house."

He raced on. "It's our Moses."

I frowned and thought hard. "But, but," I pointed out, "Our Moses is a girl!"

Our Moses was later named Lucille Doreen.

Chapter 28 Pussycat, Pussycat,
Where Have You Been?

When King George came to Edmonton, John Bidulock was in the Alberta Dragoons
Royal Escorts, 1939.

In the early part of 1939, with earphones on my head, I probed a cavity in our molar-like crystal radio, searching for CJCA. It was the clearest radio station that reached our remote farm, which was located one hundred miles northeast of Edmonton, Alberta. I suspected our teacher thought my news item was fabricated when I reported it that morning. That week, the fifth graders were responsible for current events. Although I reported news heard on our crystal radio set, I sometimes made up news items for an unprepared and shy girl friend, while we walked to school.

"Oh just say that a fishing boat is lost in the fog off the Nova Scotia shores," or "There was a small earthquake in Japan—no one was killed or hurt," or "Many people in Africa are starving." Our teacher seemed pleased that my slow friend reported at all.

That particular morning I listened to the news and reported that King George VI and Queen Elizabeth would visit Canada and that they would be in Edmonton.

"Where did you get that news?" our teacher asked with an incredulous expression on his face.

"The radio. This morning," I answered meekly. In time it became common news. The royal couple would visit Edmonton.

I knew that Edmonton was our capital city, but had never been there. In fact, I had little concept of what a "city" really was. I had never travelled beyond the hamlet of Hairy Hill, which was only twelve miles from our farm.

As the day for the royal visit approached, our teacher told us the schools would be closed, to allow children to travel to Edmonton. He would be going and there would be room for three pupils in his car. Each child was asked to give a small amount to help pay for the gas. Since there were five from my family who attended the country school, we realized we could not go. First, our parents could not afford even a small amount per child. Second, there were too many of us. Most other families had similar difficulties. Although disappointed, we were resigned to our lot and the important day was rarely mentioned thereafter.

My father, however, listened to the news regularly. He heard details of the royal visit. I'm sure he did some thinking and a lot of soul-searching. Schools were closed for the special event. He would not deny his children a most unusual learning experience.

The evening before the special day, Father silently reached a decision. He indicated that those who attended school should be ready to travel very early the following morning. I could hardly contain my excitement and although I often feared my dad, I knew he was a wonderful and caring father.

On that cool crisp June morning, we piled into the 1927 Essex and left for

Edmonton. The narrow wheels of the Essex seemed to hit every hole in the bumpy roads, but we did not complain, and sat silently with teeth clenched.

We headed west, parallel to the North Saskatchewan River, past Deep Lake School, past the exit to the Desjarlais Ferry, past Cucumber Lake, past the small town of Andrew, to Bruderheim. That was a German settlement. The name of the town meant "Brothers' Home." Father spouted off the few German words he knew: *Guten Tag* and *Guten Morgen*. He enjoyed using his very limited foreign vocabulary, and I was impressed.

After travelling through Bruderheim, we turned to a southerly direction. Fort Saskatchewan was the next town. Everyone knew the town had a jail.

When a remark like "Oh, he was sent to Fort Saskatchewan" was made, it was implied that "he went to jail." As we approached the town, we headed directly towards a high gate with heavy bars.

"That's the jail," Father pointed out.

But why were we going straight towards it? Just before we reached the gate, the road veered sharply to the left and around the compound. While my thoughts were still engrossed with the jail, I became aware of a strange sensation. It felt like we floated on air. I heard Father say, "It's so nice to drive on pavement."

So these are paved roads. How wonderful! I thought.

When we arrived in Edmonton, hundreds of people lined a prairie road running in a southeasterly direction, at an angle from a small airport. Most Edmonton

Kingsway Avenue was named after the Royal Visit of George VI in 1939.

roads were on a grid system, but not this one. We stood on the south side of the road and faced north. Beyond were shrubs and prairie grasses. In the distance behind us was a cluster of buildings, including several impressive four- or five-storey skyscrapers. That was Edmonton in 1939!

More people, including many children, now stood along both sides of the road. Everyone was given a little flag like the big one hanging above the blackboard on the front wall of our schoolroom.

We waited a long time. Then the throng seemed to stir with anticipation. Eventually motorcycle escorts and an open car slowly approached and went past.

King George VI sat on the far side. I thought he looked handsome. He smiled but mostly looked straight ahead. Queen Elizabeth smiled and waved a white-gloved hand. I was certain that she looked straight at me. In a trance I gazed at the departing royal pair. It was only after the car had rolled past that I realized the people around me were waving their flags. I waved mine too.

The royal visit was over in a few short minutes. But we did see the king and queen. It was a memorable moment for me and for Edmonton. The road the royal couple travelled is now called Kingsway Avenue. The road branching off Kingsway is named Princess Elizabeth Avenue, after the Royals' eldest daughter. Princess Elizabeth eventually became queen after her father, King George VI, died in 1952.

The trip to Edmonton to see the king and queen was a highlight in my young life. In the days following the event, my sister and I scratched an unusually long hopscotch on the packed ground between the big house and the summerhouse. As we hopped, we waved our flags and recited:

> Pussycat, Pussycat
> Where have you been?
> I've been to Edmonton
> To see the king and queen.

> Pussycat, Pussycat
> What did you there?
> I waved my union jack
> Way up in the air.

Chapter 29 An Unsolved Mystery

John Bidulock joined the RCAF in 1939 and later (in the
1970s and 1980s) led the Air Cadets in Two Hills, Alberta.

The following account is based on bits of information overheard when I was a curious child: my blurred memories of tense adult conversations regarding Harry. More than sixty years later, I still wonder, what really happened to Harry? And why did this happen to someone with so much potential? The worst part is that I will never know.

John and one of his motorbikes, 1943.

The story begins with the homesteaders in the community of Deep Lake during the horse and buggy days. And as most did not own a buggy, perhaps those days are better called the horse and wagon days.

Harry had a mediocre interest in farming. He enjoyed travelling and dabbled in sales, at a time when salesmen were almost non-existent in the community.

Harry, an only child, enjoyed occasional visits with my dad, Fred. He regarded

Road work, 1950s.

Fred as an older brother. But he also enjoyed the company of Fred's oldest son, John, whom he regarded as a younger brother. When the three met, they enjoyed discussing topics other than the usual farm fare. Their lively conversations often included world affairs and cars, world affairs because there were few others who shared their interest, and cars because they were new and exciting. And when it came to cars, they especially loved discussing engines and what made cars run.

In the mid-thirties, although money was tight, my dad bought a small truck. It was the first automobile in the community. A few years later Harry sold him a 1927 Essex that served the family well for many years. My dad was impressed with his friend's honesty and intelligence.

Some time later, Harry visited, riding a motorcycle. That whetted John's interest. He was determined that one day he too would own one.

During those early days, prior to the invention of caterpillars, bobcats or backhoes, road improvements within municipalities were done with horses and fresnos. The fresno was a large metal scoop pulled by two horses. An operator guided it using the wooden handles attached on either side of the scoop. The horses' reins were often fastened around the operator's waist because he needed both hands to manage the equipment.

A typical road improvement involved fixing low spots which otherwise remained potholes well into the summer. In this case a wooden culvert was built and positioned before the soil was built up using the fresnos.

To reduce the cost of road maintenance, rural municipalities required one day of labour per year, per quarter section, from their landowners. It is unclear to me whether the labour was donated to the municipality or if the work was in lieu of property taxes. A government foreman was in charge of the work and kept an account of the farms represented.

Harry's problems began one sunny summer day during a road maintenance session. My brother John, then in his twenties, had experience working the fresno. He would work on the road crew that day instead of his father. The road-building was only a mile from home, so at noon Mother would have a younger family member take John his lunch.

John worked hard all morning. He was delighted that Harry worked that day too. At lunchtime they sat together on the grass to eat and enjoy each other's company. Like his father, John was always impressed by his friend's intelligence and common sense, and was glad to have Harry for a friend.

When John's lunch arrived, from the north, Harry walked several hundred feet south, beyond a small hill, to retrieve his. It waited in the shade of a shrub at the crossroad. The other men who brought their lunches left them at the crossroad too.

As they ate, the two enthusiastically discussed motorcycles. However, Harry seemed disturbed by the state of his lunch. There was something about it that did not seem right. After a few bites he decided the food had a strange taste. He tried several more bites and then complained further. He could not continue. The lively conversation ended quickly. Harry clutched his stomach. Within a few short moments he became violently ill and would not continue with road-building that afternoon.

The details of Harry's condition after he left for home are sketchy. I am not sure if he went to the hospital. I have a vague recollection of an investigation by the RCMP. My family knew little of his condition. Although Fred and John often thought of Harry, they did not travel to see him, nor did Harry visit our home.

Months elapsed before the local news arrived. Harry's illness had affected his mind. He was in the mental hospital at Ponoka, some two hundred miles away.

In the meantime John had travelled to British Columbia, where he worked and purchased the long-anticipated motorcycle. On his return to Alberta he travelled through Ponoka. He wanted to show Harry his bike and ask for an opinion. John looked forward to seeing his old friend again.

Harry was delighted to see John but there was a definite change in the man. Although Harry remembered their good visits, he had moments of silence when he retreated into another world. He remembered the fateful day he became ill. He seemed convinced that someone had tampered with his lunch. The egg was not only cracked but part of the shell at one end was missing. On his departure John pledged to visit his friend as often as possible.

Then the Second World War began. John joined the RCAF. Soon after enlisting he was posted overseas. He often thought of his friend Harry when he rode the motorcycle commissioned to him in England.

Four years later, John returned to Canada and visited Harry at his first opportunity. John was extremely saddened to find the once intelligent and brilliant man completely uncommunicative. Harry failed to respond no matter how hard John tried. The two best friends had become strangers.

Many speculated on the cause of Harry's illness: "Was the food in his lunch stale? The boiled egg had a crack in it, but had it not been boiled just that morning?"

"Could Harry have contracted E-coli from bad food? Would that affect one's brain?"

"Did someone tamper with Harry's lunch? It was behind the hill and out of sight, so there was opportunity. But why would anyone harm the man? He had no known enemies."

"Did the police do a sufficient job investigating the case?"

"Or was the lunch just a red herring, a coincidence? Did Harry already have a latent illness? "

Now, sixty years later, I still wonder about Harry. He was a vibrant and fine young man. His illness was tragic.

Every now and then my thoughts drift back to the days when Harry's problems were on the lips of everyone who knew him. But the riddle remains an unsolved mystery.

Chapter 30 Farm Animals

Cow and calf, 1970.

Dad and Mother's farming days began with a yoke of oxen. Much of the initial breaking of land was done with the strong beasts. In addition, a cow and chickens were some of their early animals. As time went on, other animals were added, the most important of which were horses. Dad traded the oxen for his first team of horses. Sheep and more cows slowly joined the farm menagerie, as well as turkeys and geese. The chickens provided eggs and meat but the other poultry was raised to sell.

In late autumn, after we moved back to the big house, the cool summerhouse was used to prepare the extra turkeys and geese for market. Usually one male and about three or four females were kept for next spring's breeding. A couple of days before the day the train would travel west to Edmonton, the family pitched in to get the poultry ready.

Animals were always present at the farm, 1930–1990.

Three strong hooks were installed in the ceiling of the summerhouse. A large bucket was set below the first hook. That was where Dad did the dirty work. With expert manipulation of a fine knife, the nerve and artery were severed through the mouth. The bird fluttered just a few seconds. He quickly removed the larger feathers, then transferred the bird to a second hook, where more feathers were removed by other helpers. On the final hook the few feathers left came off. Mother did the final inspection. The birds were laid side by side on the cold table. The room was kept cool so we wore warm clothes.

During the procedure each bird was suspended by its feet. The heads were required to be left intact and drawing was not required. When geese were prepared in this fashion, the down was saved for pillows.

Four horses were necessary to pull the plough, the discs, the harrows, or the thresher. Because he was aware of the importance of horses, Dad cared for them well. During the busy season he gave them an extra measure of oats and hay and we curried them often. Horses like that.

During drought when pastures were poor, Dad limited the number of cows. The sheep pasture was an enclosure around the lake. But seventy sheep would soon nibble the grass to its roots. So Dan and Mike watched over them on the road allowance. That gave the pasture time to rejuvenate.

As a rule we had only one litter of piglets per year, but sometimes two. Much depended on the amount of grain harvested that particular year.

Cows were milked morning and evening. By age twelve, we were recruited to do the milking. Our knuckles hurt but we knew it would not last forever.

Cats controlled the mouse population. However, they were not house cats. When they wandered into the open summerhouse door for morsels of something different, Mother shooed them out. The dog, too, would saunter into the house, knowing full well he did not belong there. He wagged his tail when one of us patted his head or gave him something special off the table.

We had no real pets as city people would regard them, and yet all our animals were our pets. It seems that we were too busy and there were too many animals to give any one animal a lot of attention. Probably the closest to what might be regarded as a pet was a pup that replaced the old dog that died. He resembled a bear cub, and so was dubbed "Cubby." I think he was part German shepherd. We adored him and played with him all summer. When we left for school in the fall he missed us. One morning as we rounded the lake on our way to school, Steve spotted Cubby racing to catch up with us. Changes were made until he learned his place.

When Cubby grew and learned about the ways of the farm, he saved us the misery of a cold walk to get the cows home for milking. The cows fed and slept at a straw pile beyond the lake. At milking time Dad called out, "Na Na Na," as Cubby wagged his tail beside him.

"Go get them. Go on. Get the cows." The cows were alerted by the call. Then they saw the lone dog approach and soon headed for home with Cubby proudly following them.

A runt piglet received much attention from us even though Dad said that it would not live. Our hearts went out to the little animal.

Farm animals' deaths and accidents affected us because we regarded them as part of our family. I sadly remember the death of Frank, a dapple-grey horse. A cow reaching for bulrushes on the edge of the large lake, beyond the closer slough, got stuck in the mud. It took ropes, people, and finally the use of a horse, to get her out.

All our animals served the farm. The horses, of course, pulled the farm implements, but also provided transportation to town during the winter months. The cows gave us milk, cheese, cream, butter. When milk was plentiful during the summer months, extra cream was saved in a special five-gallon cream can and shipped to a dairy in Edmonton. The cream cans had the name of the dairy as well as the sender's name painted on them. They were set on the station platform before the train arrived. Empty cans were returned to the platform when the train travelled east.

During the early years the sheep were milked. Cheese from sheeps' milk was comparable to feta cheese. The wool gave us stockings, mittens, sweaters, quilts. Extra wool was sold or sent to Fairfield's Woollen Mills in Ontario to be converted into blankets. Old and torn woollen clothes were saved over the years and also sent to the mill for coarser blankets. As well, the calves, lambs, and pigs that Dad did not want to keep were sold.

Only one set of twin calves was born on the farm. Sheep often had twins and occasionally triplets. Mother taught a lamb to feed from a cow when its mother had triplets. Only one colt was born on the farm.

A stallion that Dad bought lasted only a few years before he was sold. He was a big horse and Nick liked to ride him when he visited friends. One day George and I decided we would ride him. We had no saddle.

"You go first," George coaxed. I was about twelve. When I mounted the big animal bareback he took off like a shot. The dog's barks spooked him. I held on to his mane but just as he galloped through an open wire gate I began to slip. I saw the gatepost below me and held on for dear life. By the time we reached the field beyond the lake, he got tired and I was finally able to control him.

"Your hair was flying," George remarked. He did not wish to ride him.

Our parents cautioned us about getting near animals that were protective of their young. Horseback riding was discouraged. Preventing accidents was foremost on our parents' minds. Doctors had to be paid.

However, one day after the children had left home, Mother was near a sow that had piglets. She wished to provide fresh straw bedding for the litter. The sow did not like her presence and attacked. With pitchfork in hand she tried to protect herself. Holding the fork horizontally she forced it into the sow's open mouth and held it there until the animal backed away. But much of the skin on the back of her hands was torn off.

For a while Father was chief cook and dishwasher. He did the milking. Amazingly, Mother's wounds healed without infection or professional medical attention.

Chapter 31 The Girls in Blue

Kathleen, Pearl and Lucille with calf. Kathleen and Pearl were often mistaken for twins, 1937.

Every coin, regardless of its denomination, had great value to homesteaders during the *dirty thirties*. To find even a one-cent coin on the street filled one's heart with joy. Everyone heard about it.

As young children, we had few opportunities to get money. We could count on two events during the year when that might become reality. Singing carols at neighbouring farm homes at Christmas generally earned us a total of almost a dollar. But we could earn more during the summer. Our family generally attended two picnics—one at nearby Sandy Lake and the second in the town of Hairy Hill.

Besides watching grown-ups play softball and meet with acquaintances, there were other attractions: races were scheduled and cash prizes given to successful competitors. That part of the picnic interested us most and we planned to participate. Practice was important so a couple of weeks before the picnics my siblings and I planned a practice program. Each evening after chores were done and the dishes cleared, before bedtime, we ran from the gate to the barn. We ran and ran. My sister Kathleen and I practised the three-legged race. We counted on it. We ran it so often that it became almost perfect. We did well at the first picnic. However, the town picnic was the big one. Many more races were scheduled with many more opportunities. We practised long and hard for that one.

The large schoolyard in Hairy Hill was a flurry of activity when we arrived. More people arrived as the afternoon wore on. In time a man with a large horn announced preparation for the races.

Kathleen and I were just over a year apart in age but I grew fast and caught up with her. Mother made our dresses from the same bolt of material so often people who did not know us thought we were twins. On the day of the picnic we wore blue dresses.

The running races were scheduled first and we did well, but the three-legged race was our forte.

"Nine and under for the three-legged race!" the horn blasted out. We fit that category and won handily.

"Twelve and under," he yelled. Again we came in first place, beating the runners-up by a good margin.

"Fifteen and under. Line up." Kathleen and I stood on the starting line and looked up at the tall girls to our left and right. Then a loud voice called again.

"Take the girls in blue out of the line. They can't run."

I looked at my sister in dismay. "Why can't we race? We are under fifteen!"

Father stood near the finish line only a short distance from the horn-blower. He knew the man—principal of the school. They were acquaintances for many years and had great chats whenever they met. They had mutual respect for each other.

"Why not?" Father asked aloud.

"Are they your girls?"

"That doesn't matter. They are under fifteen." The horn was lifted again.

"It's all right," he blared. "It's all right. They may run." We won again!

The incident stayed with me. Father knew we were going to win. Was he greedy in making his remark? Our participation was legitimate. At eight and nine years of age we should certainly be allowed to run in a fifteen and under race. We planned. We practised. We were prepared. We won. But it bothered me. . .

Whenever I remembered that particular incident, an argument that gave me solace was: Participants in the Olympics games practise a lot. They are allowed to compete again even though they won before. Yes, practice and dedication are important to an athlete. They practise unceasingly. Practice makes perfect.

Chapter 32 The Stolen Bike

We walked and we walked. We walked to a ball game. We walked to our neighbours'. We walked to the post office. Our dad had a car but he was the only one who drove it. He claimed it was a working car to be used only for absolutely necessary trips.

Nick would do something about that. He heard that a young man, hardly an acquaintance, had a bike for sale. It was priced at eight dollars. But Nick did not have eight dollars. He would gladly share the bike with us if we helped him get the money. He approached three of us who composed the middle group in our large family.

If each of us put in two dollars we could buy the bike.

Two dollars was all I had. I had earned it running races at picnics. Reluctantly I parted with it.

The bike was purchased. The boys kept their promise and taught my sister and me to ride. As we wobbled unsteadily while learning to balance, one of the boys ran alongside supporting us by holding onto the seat of the bike. With practice our confidence was bolstered and we soon were able to manage, even though it was a boy's bike with the high bar.

Our brothers rode the bike most of the time, but did not mind if my sister and I used it too.

One day Nick reported that he heard that the bike was a stolen bike. That meant the RCMP could take it away. The news made us nervous.

One Sunday two young men who were friends of the seller came to our house. I had never seen them before and they were only casual acquaintances of my brothers. While they visited they complimented my brothers on the nice bike. Then one asked if he might try it out. He rode it over the hill and took his time getting back.

Later we heard the police were looking for a stolen bike. It was bad news. The police would check the serial numbers on the few bikes in the community. The news prompted Dad to check the serial number on our bike. He was horrified to learn that the number had been filed off. Who did it, and when?

Because the police had no search warrant they could not legally come to our house and confiscate the bike.

One Sunday afternoon our older brother Dan borrowed our bike to go to Deep Lake School to play ball. He returned home on foot. The RCMP had met him on the road, questioned him about the bike, and took it. Now Dan was in real trouble with our group of four. He was responsible for losing our bike and we let him know it.

Dan was determined to compensate us. He knew that he would not get anywhere by approaching the seller who had sold us a stolen bike. But he heard that the seller's mother was going to take hogs to town on market day. He went to town with his dad, approached the woman after she sold the hogs, and retrieved the eight dollars that we paid for the bike.

The following summer the rusted bike continued to lean against a building in a fenced enclosure at the police station.

Kathleen on bike in front of 1927 Essex; niece Judy on doorstep, 1942.

Chapter 33 Shots in the Blueberry Patch

Picking strawberries. Dan, Mother, Gladys, Pearl with basin, Nick, George, Mike, 1937.

Homesteads near the North Saskatchewan River were not only picturesque but often, to the family's delight, provided wild berries throughout the summer.

The virgin land, untouched by extensive cultivation, offered landscapes that would be a painter's delight. But although the scenery was most beautiful, the land was not conducive to the homesteaders' hopes, namely, farming.

Like most neighbouring homesteads, my father's land had rocks. It had rocks of every size and shape—round rocks, long rocks, flat rocks, odd-shaped rocks. Although rocks were picked and thrown along a fence line, more surfaced during successive ploughing.

One could never get rid of them all. A lone rock almost two metres in diameter lay on our hay field, as if rolled there by a mighty giant practising bowling. Because some rocks were too cumbersome to remove with horses, if the farmer could afford it, dynamite was bought and used to reduce them to manageable size. On occasion, the farmyard sounds were broken by the unfamiliar sound of a distant explosion.

Dad's chosen land appealed to his love of landscape—water, woods, ravines, sloughs, and meadows that were often embraced by fluffy white clouds in an azure sky. To open one's arms, feel the gentle breeze on the face, and look up at the heavens brought a feeling of joy and peace.

Another feature of the land that appealed to Dad was the large variety of wild berries that seemed to grow anywhere and everywhere—wild raspberries, strawberries, saskatoons, chokecherries, currants, gooseberries, dewberries, cranberries, and blueberries.

"Truly, one could live off the land," Dad surmised.

In June wild strawberries began the berry-picking season, followed by other varieties of berries throughout the summer and well into the fall. The area where blueberries grew was a special blessing because it was only a short walk from our home.

During the late summer and early fall, we younger children picked blueberries. Day after day, berries were picked and eaten and preserved and picked and eaten and preserved.

One day, as the summer progressed into fall and we were getting tired of berry picking, we met one of the neighbours' children who suggested we go to a spot quite distant from home.

Peggy was somewhat older than we were, but she was glad to join us. We did not particularly want her along because she was bossy. She came up with ideas about everything, controlled every situation, and took great pleasure in manipulating us.

The previous summer she lured me from the group to an area where cranberries grew. I was only six or seven. Before we began to pick she dug into a pocket and withdrew a filthy rag that had something concealed in it. She invited me to sit near her as she unfolded the rag and exposed cigarette-rolling paper and a wad of tobacco. What was she up to? I watched her in wonderment. I was confused and somewhat disgusted. Yes, most men rolled their own and smoked, but I had never seen a female smoke. Cigarettes were not meant for women and girls.

As she began to deposit tobacco onto the paper, a horse-drawn wagon rattled past on a trail that was within sight. Peggy became nervous. The tobacco slipped to the ground and got lost in the cranberries. She abandoned her project. Then

Miss Bossy looked at me with piercing eyes and made me promise that I would not tell anyone as long as I lived. (Now, by telling this story, I have broken the promise.)

On that day in the blueberry patch, Peggy offered advice.

"I have an idea," she began as we headed towards the *big curve*—the farthest berry patch from home. The curve, a large bend in the road, enclosed a steeply sloped area of trees, bushes, and berries. It enabled travel from a high elevation to a lower level, which ended near the riverbank. From the curve we could see the river. We could hear the rapids, and if we squinted, we could see beyond the water a small group of farm buildings set on a small plateau. They were the only sign of civilization from our vantage point on the top of the curve.

Blueberries were plentiful in the curve because we had not wandered this far from home to pick them before.

"Yes. It's a good idea," Peggy repeated thoughtfully. "We'll set all the bowls here in a row. Then we'll all fill one bowl and empty it into the others until all are full. Won't that be fun?" she added enthusiastically.

Peggy's idea was different but at that moment I did not question the fact that her bowl was much larger than any of ours nor that she was one person helping our family whereas three of us were helping her.

It was rather fun contributing our handfuls of berries to the common bowl and then watching it fill the others.

After Peggy's bowl and one other were full, the picking abruptly stopped.

A loud bang shattered the silence in the blueberry patch. It startled us. We stood rooted to our spots. I thought it came from the woods on the lower side of the curve.

"What's that?" my older sister asked, clutching her chest. We held our breath. No one dared move.

Was someone shooting at us? Why would anyone want to do that? The thought of safety never occurred to us while picking berries. We never feared being without an adult. Except for birds and insects flying about, there were few sounds in the berry patch.

We stood silent and motionless for a long time. Then Peggy crouched to the ground.

Another shot shattered the silence. We crouched down near her. Then, in a little more than a whisper, she broke the silence. "It's my father! I think he came back. I think he's angry with us." She became extremely agitated.

Peggy's father's land was one of the poorest in the area. With inadequate farm equipment and only two horses, he could not feed his family off the land. So he worked away from home and brought back staples and money whenever he could.

Berrypicking was enjoyed by many, 1945.

"Let's grab our berries and run!" Peggy whispered. But the bowls were at the bottom of the slope.

"You go get them," she dictated, pointing at me. I shook. No! I could not move! Then my older sister took my hand and together we crouched low and slowly crept downward. As we advanced I did not dare look around lest I get shot. But through the corner of my eye I was quite certain that I saw a man in the woods near the sharpest bend in the road.

"Oh no!" I whispered in dismay. "My sweater is hanging on a branch over there."

"We can't go for it now. You grab the empty bowls." My life, I decided, was more important than a sweater.

We hurried home. Peggy decided to run ahead to tell her mother.

"Peggy's father was shooting at us. We were picking blueberries in the curve. We heard two shots. They came very near to us." I talked on non-stop.

"Peggy said her father came back and is angry. And I saw him in the woods. He had on a black coat and was hiding behind bushes."

Our parents and older siblings were in the house as I rattled on. Strange smiles appeared on their faces. Why were they smiling? That was serious. How could they smile at such a dangerous time? Rather than look concerned, Father laughed.

"Peggy's father would never do that. When he comes home he brings the family food. He left only a couple of weeks ago but if he's back already, he wouldn't hurt his family."

"But I saw a man in black. He was right there where the road turns downward. And we heard the shots. They came right past us. It's good we weren't hurt. And my sweater—it's still on a branch there," I raced on non-stop.

Father scratched his head thoughtfully. To ease my fear and retrieve the sweater, an older brother would go back with me. I felt safe with my big brother near.

As we approached the curve I shivered. By this time the man might be on his way up to confront his family. I held on to Dan's pants.

"He was down there in the curve. We have to be quiet. Right there. Right there. See. Right there. We must be careful. Oh dear! He's still there!"

I heard Dan laugh.

"You silly little girl. That black thing is not a man. It's just a burnt-out stump. Come see. That's not a man." A black stump stood partly concealed by foliage.

"Well, who shot at us?"

Just then a shot broke the silence. I shook and hid behind Dan.

"See! See! He's at it again. Let's run home."

"You silly girl. Is that what you heard? That came from across the river where a farmer is blasting rocks and the water carries the sound across, so it's loud. Your imagination is beyond me. Come on, enough of this nonsense. Let's go home."

With one hand clutching my sweater and the other holding on to Dan's hand, I laboured up the steep incline.

Chapter 34 Food at the Farm

Maria peeling potatoes. Cream separator is airing out on top of Maytag gas-powered washing machine, 1957.

When the call *La mincari! Venits la mincari!* came from the summerhouse, hungry family members dropped what they were doing and hurried to the house.

Breakfasts were always porridge, with pancakes too if Mother had time to prepare the batter. Her batter was made with fresh eggs and a yogurt type of sour milk (*kishlac*). The pancakes fried in homemade butter (*oont*) were thick and fluffy, often with a crispness that made them most tasty. Eggs were rarely cooked for breakfast. We drank milk (*lapti*) or cocoa, never coffee.

Zoupa at lunchtime was a constant, often eaten with bread (*keeta*) and cheese (*brinza*). If a chicken (*gyena*) was cooked, it was generally boiled rather than roasted so the broth could be used for the soup.

Depending on the situation, dinners varied. We generally had potatoes, boiled or fried; cheese; or meat. Sometimes it was a large pot of dumplings (*keeroshki*) filled with a mixture of homemade cheese, eggs, and chopped onions (*chapa*), never with potatoes like *perogies*. Sometimes the dumplings were sautéed in sour cream with dill and green onions. For a dumpling supper the family sat around the table with fork in hand and ate right from the common pot. There were few dishes to wash after such a meal.

Once when Gladys and Helen were in charge of the cooking, while Mother was entertaining unexpected visitors, the girls were draining the dumplings when a good portion of them slipped into the slop pail. Although the animals would relish them, it meant that there would not be enough for the family dinner. The girls were reluctant to tell Mother. When the few dumplings were ready, Mother offered some to the guests. While she insisted they have more, Gladys and Helen wished that she would stop. After the guests left the family sat down to a less than "eat all you want" meal!

Desserts in the summer were usually freshly picked strawberries, saskatoons, raspberries, or blueberries. Often a sprinkle of sugar and cream were put on top. In winter dessert was mainly preserved berries.

In the early days very little food was bought. No food produced on the farm had preservatives or additives. We had no idea of the vitamin or mineral content, nor were we even aware of vitamins and minerals. However, our vegetables would have been regarded as organic.

Cows were milked twice a day by hand, and milk provided us with cream, butter, cheese, and yogurt. For cottage cheese, the skim milk congealed when set in a pot for a day at room temperature. It was then cooked at a low temperature. During that process, curds separated from the whey. Because we did not have a colander or sieve, the curds were poured into a clean cotton sugar bag and hung from a high spot. The whey dripped, leaving the curds quite dry. The resulting curds were mixed with sour cream to make cottage cheese. Cheese made to last the winter was usually made from whole milk in the fall when, according to our parents, the milk was of a richer quality. That cheese had an extra important ingre-

A meal with family and neighbours, 1950.

dient added to the milk before it was set to congeal. Mother bought rennet tablets and added just the slightest fraction of a tablet to the batch. After the cheese dripped in the bag, it was put into a crock or small wooden barrel. A layer of cotton, a well-scrubbed board, and finally a heavy, clean stone put on top of the cheese squeezed any further whey to the surface where it was sponged off. The crock was often kept in the unheated summerhouse during the winter. I remember chopping the frozen cheese to get enough for our meal. The dairy products and eggs provided most of the protein we needed when we had no meat.

When Mother killed two chickens on a summer day, one was cooked and the other plucked and saved in the water pail lowered to just above the surface of the water in the well to keep cool. It would be cooked the following day. A cold-storage dugout in the side of the bank near the granary kept food partially frozen most of the winter months. That was where pork, mutton, and beef were kept frozen all winter and often well into the spring. Dad built a teepee-type structure where he smoked the bacon and hams. However, in the summer, chicken and the occasional fish caught in the river were about the only meat we had. Some neighbours bought bologna but our parents never did.

Mushrooms were often included in our diet: morels in the early spring, red-tops that grew under spruce in the blueberry patch, and mushrooms that appeared in the fall after the first frost, near the base of trees in the pasture. If they were plentiful, fall mushrooms were pulled apart into thin slivers and dried for the winter.

Now and then Mother soaked dry peas, beans, or broad beans overnight and cooked them the next day. During the fall and early winter, vegetables were available—turnips, carrots, beets, and parsnips—but they rarely lasted beyond Christmas. Shredded cabbage allowed to process provided us with sauerkraut.

Bread was the filler. It was eaten with all meals except breakfast. In the summer bread was baked, fifteen or twenty loaves at once, in an outdoor oven. In the winter, smaller batches were baked in the stove oven. Flour (*fayina*) was milled from our own wheat which Dad took to the Vegreville flour mill. Because he travelled with horses, the 35-mile trip had to be done over two days.

School sandwiches were often made with jam, cheese, or peanut butter. Dad bought the peanut butter in large pails. To make it go farther, each morning we mixed some peanut butter with milk in a bowl. That made it easier to spread on the bread as well.

I remember Mother rolling out large flat circles of dough and laying them on sheets to dry. When they were dry, she sliced them thinly for pasta. About the only canned food we bought was the occasional can of tomatoes. The empty cans were saved for planting geraniums.

Maria, Sandy, and cat with prize pumpkin, 1975.

A large family needed much food. Therefore, everyone pitched in to help get it: milking, weeding, harvesting, picking berries, separating milk, churning cream into butter. Some of the foods that were bought included salt, sugar, yeast, baking powder, cornmeal, and rolled oats. Now and then a box of apples was bought. Although we were often hungry when we set up stooks or did other strenuous work, I don't remember ever going to bed hungry.

Mother did not know about cholesterol. She did not know about calories, and she did not know about vitamins or minerals that were important for one's health. But by the grace of God, and her intuition and determination to provide for her family, she succeeded. She expected help from the family and, as a result, each of us was introduced to life's responsibilities.

Note: The Romanian words in italics are not spelled correctly but are written in the hope that they will be easy to pronounce.

Chapter 35 Manna

"The firewood must be saved for winter. Do not use it for the oven."
So horses were hitched to the wagon and driven along the wooded road allowance that surrounded the lake. Deadwood—fallen trees and branches—soon filled the wagon and were then deposited near the outdoor oven.

The oven was always there. I did not witness the construction of the long igloo-like structure made, not from ice, but from clay.

Despite the sandy make-up of soil on the homestead, Father was both delighted and grateful when he discovered a seam (a layer) of clay east of the gran-

The baking tradition continues. Pearl Murray, 1970.

Nick with outdoor oven in background, 1945.

ary. It provided caulking that mostly filled cracks between logs in buildings but was also used to build the outdoor oven—a huge piece of pottery.

Once the dough had been pampered all day—punched, pulled, slapped, and shaped in a large basin, then finally moulded into round large balls and set into round pans—it was time for a roaring fire to be built in the outdoor oven. The fire would heat the adobe interior to a high degree. When the oven was very hot and the bread in pans had risen, an alarm was heard throughout the barnyard:

"It's time to carry the loaves!"

At that point it was necessary to work quickly lest the oven begin cooling off. All available hands rushed the risen bread from the summerhouse to the oven (one loaf at a time), where Mother had already scraped the live embers to the mouth of the oven. With a flat, long paddle each pan was positioned on the floor of the hot oven. The layer of bread seemed to consist of white puff-balls but would soon change to a golden brown. The opening was closed with a metal sheet to contain the heat within. Then the helping hands returned to their work. As we worked, some in the garden and others in the barn, the aroma of baking bread permeated the barnyard. Our mouths watered as we looked forward to enjoying the fresh bread.

Like manna from above, the warm bread from the clay oven was broken into pieces and slathered with home-churned butter. It tasted heavenly. The family ate, enjoyed, and thrived. Bread baked in a clay oven cannot be beat. It's very special.

Chapter 36 Wild Animals Near the Farm

Early farm days witnessed many wild animals. Bears were often seen or encountered. Other animals were about and we saw them from time to time, always excitedly reporting the encounter to the rest of the family.

We occasionally saw skunks, rabbits, weasels, chipmunks, hedgehog (seen only once), porcupines, coyotes, muskrats, and lots of gophers. In more recent times beavers adopted an area along the river.

When I was small, Dad saw a rabbit that was infested with big lumps, most noticeably on its ears and face. Few rabbits were seen after that. It is possible the disease reduced their numbers.

As the settlers moved in, the bears disappeared. Interestingly, almost a century later as the people population declined, the bears made a comeback. John saw them when he ran the farm. They clawed a granary that was in the field. One day around that time Jerry (Steve's son) flew low over the farm and saw two bears near the spring on the west quarter. He said that he wished someone were with him to share the exciting moment. As they ran across the field of grain east of the creek, apparently frightened by the roar of the plane, the lighter coloured one's fur appeared silver.

Adeline recalled spotting a lynx. Both she and Beth, while teenagers, were bringing the cows home from the west quarter. The animal was in a tree near the spring about the same area as Jerry's sighting of bears. As the girls followed the cows, they kept looking back, fearing that the lynx might attack.

One of the boys, Steve or Nick, came home one day smelling like a skunk. A neighbour at our place suggested that to rid his clothes of the odour, they should be buried under soil for a day or so. He claimed that washing did not remove the odour.

I remember some of our chickens found dead in the coop. Their necks bore puncture marks—a weasel's attack. One of our dogs appeared at the door with his nose resembling a pincushion. Father forced a block of wood into the dog's mouth to prevent him from biting and with pliers removed the quills. The dog was a slow learner; sometime later he was attacked again. But that time there were only three or four quills to remove.

George and owl, 1957.

Coyotes often howled at night, likely wishing to steal a chicken or two. But the dog's barking kept them at bay. Our sleep was interrupted so often we just ignored the barking and slept well.

In recent years deer have often been seen in many areas on the farm.

There were frogs in the lake, warty toads in the garden, salamanders in cool, dark places, and garter snakes anywhere and everywhere. I remember Nick and Steve killed a garter snake. They looped the dead snake over a fence but the end of its tail continued to move. They were told by older folk that the tail would move until the sun went down. That kept us checking on the snake all afternoon. Beth recalls waking up in shock after a nap in the summerhouse. A garter snake entered the open door and slithered across the floor.

Except for robins, there were always a variety of birds around the farm. The absence of robins was likely because the farm was sandy and there were no earthworms in the soil. Bluebirds built their nests in the tall can on the binder which held two balls of twine during grain-cutting time. It had a hole in it that made it resemble a birdhouse. By harvest time the eggs were hatched and the birds gone.

Other birds included hawks, lots of owls, partridges, crows, and meadowlarks. Barn swallows came only after the big barn was built. The lake supported a variety of ducks, herons, blackbirds, and snipes. Sometimes migrating birds, Canada geese, or cranes stopped at the lake or on the fields of grain.

Two different winters a grey goose and then a snow goose were left behind in migration and spent the winter with the farm geese. After feeding with the farm geese all winter, they disappeared in the spring when birds travelled north again.

Chapter 37 A Sweet Reward

It was a sad day. The view before me—the lakes, the trees, and fields—did not provide the solace that I sought. All was a blur in my tear-filled eyes. As well, I felt limp and dizzy. I searched for a scapegoat, someone to blame for my misfortune. But I could not point my finger at anyone. Still, it was not fair.

Deep Lake country school had closed its doors for the summer holidays. Now my siblings and I would spend the summer on the farm. We would help with the many chores and begin to prepare for the long, cold winter, a mere four months hence.

We would not see our schoolmates during the summer, but we would not miss them too much. Our large family provided ample company. From morning until evening we worked, we talked, and we laughed. We argued, we complained, and we teased.

Older members of the family had already left home. My two oldest brothers, John and Dan, joined the Royal Canadian Air Force and my oldest sister Gladys had a job away from home. Consequently, the rest of us pushed a little harder to accomplish the work of those who had already left the nest.

The war caused concern and sleepless nights for the parents of our fighting men. Would they return safely? How long would they be gone? When would the war end?

The war also caused worry on the home front. There were shortages of staples. Rationing was in effect. Although we were mostly self-sufficient on the farm, some household goods still had to be bought.

Our farm had no electricity, so freezing the garden produce and berries was out of question. Sugar was needed to preserve the fruit, but it was a rationed commodity. In order to reduce our need for store-bought sugar, our parents ordered honeybees and the honey supplemented our meagre sugar reserve.

We looked forward to two single outings each summer. In mid-July the family would attend a sports day, a picnic we called it, at nearby Sandy Lake. Later, a larger picnic would be held in the town of Hairy Hill.

I looked forward to these outings because I might see a school friend. But more importantly, these were events where I might earn a few precious coins.

In the cool of the evening, after chores were done and the dinner dishes were washed, three of my siblings and I trained for the athletic events. We ran the length of the garden—from the main gate to the barn. Then my sister Kathleen and I practised the three-legged race.

At the Sandy Lake picnic, I entered two running events for girls—the "twelve and under" and the "fifteen and under." I won cash prizes each time. My sister and I ran the three-legged race twice and won both. I took my earnings to my father.

"This is for you," I said. Because I seldom left the farm, I had little opportunity to spend the money. However, I kept two nickels for two ice-cream cones—one for Mother and one for me.

I looked up into my father's misty eyes. He accepted the money reluctantly. I saw the emotion in his face—a mixture of pride, of happiness and sadness, all in one. The Good Lord knew that times were difficult.

"You can buy sugar for Mom," I said. "She has a few coupons left."

Several weeks later, I heard my parents discuss the need to buy binder twine. The five-gallon can for cream was almost full and ready for shipping. That would help pay for the cord. Although we produced much of our food and made most of our clothes, binder twine simply had to be bought.

My success at the Sandy Lake picnic inspired me to train harder for the Hairy Hill races. I was confident I could run more races and earn even more prize money.

I could pick and sell blueberries. Mother could take them to the G.M. General Store. Mrs. G.M. was always interested in blueberries and her husband was one of the most successful businessmen in the small town.

The day before the picnic had arrived. I looked forward to my annual trip to Hairy Hill. In the morning, Kathleen and I left for the blueberry patch, only a half-mile away. We returned for soup at noon and then headed back for more.

A neighbour's daughter joined us. It was late afternoon when our pails were full. As we made our way homeward, our friend suggested that we attack the Black Jacket wasps. Black Jackets are vicious brutes. They are larger than yellow hornets and their stings are much more severe. I was not going to tangle with wasps, so I offered to watch our berries and observe the battle from a safe distance.

Both girls found stout sticks.

"One, two, three, go!" The ammunition was hurled at the wasps' nest. The attackers ducked behind low bushes as a swarm of angry wasps mounted their defence. Although I was what seemed like miles away, I felt a sudden stinging pain on my forehead—right between my eyes.

When we arrived home, I was aware of some swelling on my forehead, but it was not bad at all. Surely, it would not interfere with the following day's outing.

The next morning I awoke feeling groggy. As I made my way to the summer-house, I was greeted with laughter and teasing. Fingers pointed at me and loud taunting voices yelled, "Look at that!"

"Ha, ha."

"She looks like a jack o' lantern!"

"It's the man in the moon!"

I rushed to the little mirror that hung on the wall. A puffy round face with two slits for eyes looked back at me.

"Oh no! This can't be! Not today! Please. Not today!"

I looked again and was consoled by the fact that both sides of my face were equally swollen. There are many people with fat faces, I thought. I could still go to the picnic. Folks there will just think that my face is normally fat and that's just the way I am.

That morning as the family sat around the long table eating breakfast, the discussion centred on which one of my older brothers, Nick or Steve (both in their later teens), would stay at home, to keep an eye on the farm. After much discussion my brothers' arguments swayed my parents' thinking. Although I was only twelve, I should be able to care for the farm, especially since George, who was nine, would miss the picnic too. He had an infected toe. Surely the two of us would be capable of looking after matters at the farm, my brothers argued. They won their case.

I ran out of the summerhouse and sat on the steps, in front of the big house. The splashing and honking of the geese and ducks on the lake did not amuse me that morning. The beautiful view of fields, trees, and lakes failed to pique my appre-ciation for the beauty of nature. A heart-gripping sadness filled my soul. I could not go to Hairy Hill. I would not run the races. My sister would not have a partner for the three-legged race. I could not help my father with my earnings. Would he have enough money for the binder twine?

My older brothers were elated. That morning they obeyed my mother's every command. They gladly looked after extra chores to make my day easier. But I did not appreciate any of it. Still in a state of shock, I heard lists of duties directed at me: ". . . check garden . . . cream separator . . . wash floor . . . cows . . . soak . . . soak . . . soak George's foot twice . . . at least twice . . . and . . . and . . . and . . ."

Except for the occasional honks of geese, or the bleating of lambs, an eerie silence fell over the farmyard. George and I were alone.

"Come tie this for me," George called. He held two narrow strips of inner tube rubber and a short Y-shaped branch. He stretched one end of the elastic around one arm of the Y.

"Tie the string real good. Three more," he said.

What was the list of chores Mother spelled out, I wondered? I could not remember. Every morning the cream separator was dismantled and washed. I would do that first. The breakfast dishes were still on the table. I would wash them next.

But first a basin full of warm water had to be prepared for George's infected toe. A wooden box just outside the door would be his stool.

"Sit here and soak your foot. You don't want to get blood poisoning," I commanded.

The morning passed quickly. After lunch, a second basin full of water was prepared.

"Here. Take this outside to the box. Soak your foot while I wash the floor."

George took the basin and limped out the door. In an instant, he rushed back in, splashing water over the floor.

"Eek! I'm not going out there," he screamed. "The 'Black Jacks' are all over the place!"

"What do you mean?" I asked. I looked out the open door.

The sky was dark with flying insects. It was a shocking sight. I trembled, but the swirling mass did not look like Black Jackets to me.

"It's a swarm!" I shouted. "The bees are swarming! Oh dear. We will lose our bees. Mother and Dad won't be happy about that."

We watched in horror. We were mesmerized. Eventually the buzzing sound waned. Fewer bees now flew about.

"Look!" George yelled, pointing towards the gate. The bees had seemed to congregate on a shrub near the gate. A mass of ever-moving insects clung to a branch. It grew bigger and bigger and then its weight bent the branch until it almost touched the ground.

I remembered the swarm of the previous summer. My parents saved those bees. Later, they happily discussed the nature of swarming bees. The old queen leaves the hive when a new one hatches. She leaves with a goodly number of bees. They fly about, then settle to rest. After a brief recess the queen takes wing again. Her troops follow. The colony may travel many miles before it stops to find a new home in a hollow log, or a cave. I calculated that the bees could be saved if they were caught during the rest period.

"Now!" I called aloud. "If we want to save them, it must be done now!" My eyes fell on a large wooden box. "This might do."

George scowled at me. "You can't go there! They will sting you and your face will be twice as big."

I ran to the shed for the beekeepers' mask and gloves. With box in hand, I crouched and moved gingerly towards the gate. The squirming mass caused me to shudder, as I remembered the sting of the previous evening.

The bees did not attack. They practically ignored me. I drew closer and slipped the box under the drooping clump and gently turned the open side up.

"Look for a cover," I yelled to George. A few moments later he hobbled part way towards me with two short lengths of board.

"That should do fine."

There were bees now in, on, and around the box. We wondered about the open spaces between the boards on the sides and top of the box. But as we watched from a safe distance, it appeared as though the bees were accepting their new home.

"Oh good," I said gratefully. "Mother wanted to check the hive during the week, but she was always so busy. She would have seen the new queen about to hatch and would have destroyed it. Then there wouldn't have been a swarm."

It was time to bring the cows home for milking. The floor did not get washed. George did not soak his foot a second time. But we saved the bees. That was more rewarding than running races at Hairy Hill. It was a happy day after all.

Chapter 38 Lick It Up

Maria's first beehive in the garden was unpopular. She moved it the next year, 1943.

Every time I used honey, I remembered the respect that my mother had for the lowly honeybee. If the honey dripped, I quickly licked it up, as Mother had taught me.

During the Second World War when household staples, including sugar, were rationed, our parents introduced honeybees to our already diverse mixed farm. Initially beekeeping was a novelty, and both my parents were involved in bee care. However, as time went on, Dad was less interested. Mother, on the other hand, took to it with a passion and eventually became the principal beekeeper. Although she developed an understanding and avid interest in the new venture, she became especially intrigued by the humble insect itself.

Mother quickly learned to identify the different groups of bees within the colony. There were the honey gatherers, the security guards, the cell builders, the nursery workers, and the house cleaners. However, the easiest to identify were the large, furry drones and of course the lone and unusually long queen bee.

The queen was the most important bee in the hive, laying the eggs that sustained the colony's population. On the queen's maiden flight, the drones followed her. They mated, and she then laid fertile eggs for the rest of her life. Afterwards, the lazy drones enjoyed a carefree existence, eating the honey produced by the rest of the hard-working hive. However, if a new queen hatched, they were ready to do their duty on her maiden flight, and the cycle continued.

Once Mother learned about the drones, she began to check the bees with scissors in hand and destroyed as many drones as she could see. The cleaning crew gladly removed the carcasses of the free-loaders. As well, when an elongated cell appeared in the nursery, she knew that a new queen was in the making and destroyed it too.

When a new queen hatched, the old queen would leave, taking about half the bees with her. If the hive swarmed, it meant fewer bees, which meant less honey. Therefore it was important to check the hive regularly.

Mother marvelled as each work group performed its duties in a smooth manner. She wished her large family worked in silent unison like the bees. She wondered how the bee chores were meted out so efficiently and peacefully.

Mother also marvelled at their hard work. Workers came to the hive loaded with pollen and nectar. They gathered honey from many Alberta flowers including clover, roses, daisies, and thistles, and Mother developed a genuine respect for their industriousness.

She was unhappy when her children were careless with the precious golden syrup. They enjoyed slathering slices of freshly baked bread with peanut butter and then dribbling honey on top. If the honey dripped onto a plate or on the table, Mother would say, "Lick it up clean. Do you know that a bee must make a hundred trips to the field to gather that drop of honey? Lick it up!"

Mother's instructions stayed with me. Every time that I used honey I thought of my mother and I licked up every drop!

Chapter 39 Curls Have a Mind of Their Own

Nick, 1945.

Since time eternal, hair has been regarded as an important aspect of making a fashion statement. Throughout the centuries, hairstyles have constantly changed, and to be in vogue, people have changed with the new fashion.

When my brother Nick started at our country school, he discovered that the girls were great targets for his favourite pastime: teasing. During his teens, however, he suddenly changed his thinking. He began to like girls. He wished to change his image, hoping the girls might forgive and forget, hoping the girls might like him too.

"How can I change their feelings towards me?" he wondered. He decided to start by changing his hairstyle.

Nick had inherited a head of beautiful curls—brown, with just the slightest tinge of red. The most likely source of this gift was my maternal grandfather, who had bright red curly hair. Those of us with straight hair envied Nick and the few other family members who were endowed with natural curls.

However, when Nick was in his teens, men's hairstyles changed. The hair was slicked back and plastered down with a product called Brylcreem. Pictures in the magazines and catalogues showed men with sleek hair. Bill, our neighbour, had straight hair, and wore the new style with ease. He was popular with the girls. Nick noticed and decided to do something about his curly locks.

Late one evening, Nick shampooed his hair in the washbasin. With determination, he combed it back and held it down with the palms of his hands, watching the futile effort in the small mirror hanging above the washstand. Even before he removed the comb after a backward stroke, the curls returned. At last he combed his wet hair backwards, plastered it with Brylcreem, and quickly tied on a kerchief to keep it in place. He was pleased with the effort. If his hair dried in that position, surely it would comply with his wishes. He retired for the night.

The following morning most of the family was at the kitchen table, having porridge, when Nick, his head still kerchief-bound, came down the stairs. He hurried to the little mirror. Several pairs of inquisitive eyes watched curiously, as Nick carefully removed the kerchief. He smiled with satisfaction. Except for a few little curls behind his ears and along the back of his head, the experiment had worked. He joined the family for breakfast.

As Nick ate, however, little clumps of hair escaped their prison. They wanted to be free. They needed to be free, and by the time Nick left for school, his severe new image had softened. He returned to the lovable brother we knew, and we liked Nick better that way: the way God had created him.

Nick, Dan with Philip Semenuik, 1943.

Chapter 40 Christmas Presents

At Christmas we remembered the birth of Jesus two thousand years ago. It had long been a joyful time of year. But throughout the centuries, the celebrations had changed. The emphasis had changed. The meaning had changed.

In the 1930s, the period known as the *dirty thirties*, I was a pupil at the country school at Deep Lake. Each year repeated the previous one as Christmas drew near. The teacher put our names into a box and each child drew out a name. The name was to be kept a secret. My young mind told me that this was Christmas. The day of the concert was Christmas. The giving and receiving of one single gift was Christmas. The whole student body from grade one to grade eight, generally numbering near forty, and taught by one teacher, was excited.

Money was scarce during the thirties. No assistance from the government, such as family allowance, existed. The homesteaders carried on. Those early and difficult times were a beautiful and peaceful part of my life.

Christmas for me was the school concert and the anticipation of giving and receiving a present. The one gift was a surprise that brought happiness and contentment.

The cost of each was limited to fifty cents and often the gifts were purchased through the Eaton's catalogue.

Before the concert a tree was set up in the school and presents, often wrapped in brown paper, were put under the tree. On the day of the concert we had last-minute rehearsals and were dismissed early. When we returned in the evening with our parents, we noticed a large boxful of many brown bags under the tree besides the gifts from fellow students.

At the end of the concert a noise was heard at the back door—hollering and the wild ringing of the school bell. "Ho, ho, ho. Merry Christmas. Merry Christmas, boys and girls." In his bag Santa Claus carried more brown paper bags.

I shivered with excitement when Santa arrived and shivered more when my name was called and a gift handed to me. Then I received a paper bag that contained an apple or two, an orange, peanuts, and candies. I was delighted. We had little fruit during the winter. This was special.

Our dad generally went to town with horses and sleigh before Christmas for supplies that Mother needed. He brought back a bagful of candy that he bought for twenty-five cents. We were so pleased when Dad offered each of us a candy on the occasional evening, especially when we were good.

Those days I believed that singing carols and giving gifts was a celebration of the anniversary of the birth of Jesus. But as I became older I realized that not only do we remember His birth by giving and receiving, but also that God gave us a gift at that special time many years ago. "For God so loved the world that he *gave* His only begotten Son . . ." John 3:16. That was the *ultimate* gift. It was given to the whole world with love. God's love.

Snow on the hills. Watercolour, 1999.

Chapter 41 Our Barn and Sawmill

Dan, Mike and John splitting firewood, 1935

Even before a twister removed the roof from the little barn and deposited it on the ground next to the building, my father had set up a sawmill near the entrance to the pasture. As we brought the cows home for milking we passed piles of squared-off logs loosely stacked to dry out. The older boys helped Dad saw off four sides on each log. But we young children did not question it.

The small barn stood east of where the big barn now stands. Each summer the small loft under its steep roof was filled with hay and green-feed. A trap door above the manger allowed the hay to be dropped into the manger for the cows and horses.

When as a small child I first heard the story of the birth of Jesus, I pictured Him born in a barn like our small barn and laid in a manger like ours. It was in the small barn's manger that we found George, just a little fellow of three or four, fast asleep after a long and desperate search for him by the whole family. (By the way, George was born on Christmas Day!)

When the twister removed the roof it seemed to be a definite sign that we needed a new barn. Fortunately, the logs were ready.

Dad, in spite of only four years of formal education, likely did a lot of thinking and planning. The building he planned would be a major undertaking.

The war was upon us before the building was begun. John and Dan were both in the RCAF. Mike died two years before war was declared. Nick, in his later teens, helped now and then. Steve was in Hairy Hill taking his high school and then working for the Imperial Hardware and Lumber Company. And George, also in Hairy Hill, was just in Junior High. So Dad worked on the barn alone.

Large rocks that had been thrown along fence-lines while breaking land were now hauled home and used for the foundation. The stacks of logs near the sawmill grew smaller as the walls of the barn pushed upward.

Nick told me that the huge curved trusses were erected using ropes and the help of neighbours. I wondered how that was done. I was living in Hairy Hill attending high school when that part of the barn was being completed and did not see it take place.

During a visit to the farm, Stan (my niece's husband) and I studied the structure and came up with two theories on how the trusses, almost one and a half times

Hay was heaved into the loft by fork before balers were invented. Sketch, 1980.

Sawmill, 1937.

as high as the lower part of the barn, were positioned after the log walls had been completed. We speculated that Dad might have built the loft floor after completing the lower structure. Then the trusses could have been built on that floor. With ropes, each truss may have been pulled to an upright position. A second theory was that the trusses were built in the barn, positioned upside down and then pivoted 180 degrees to an upright position with the use of ropes.

Later I spoke with Kathleen. She was at home during that time. According to her memory, the trusses were built on the ground and hoisted up with ropes and manpower.

Because the barn stood alone at that time with no fences or sheds attached to it, Dad could work from all sides.

During the war the country's economy improved. Dad bought boards, shingles, and siding for his barn. As in all barns, trap doors were designed to push the hay from the loft directly into the mangers. A door on the west end of the loft was the only way to get hay into the loft. The hayrack full of loose hay was stationed below the door and the hay was then heaved into the loft with forks. Helpers in the loft threw the hay to the far end until it reached the rafters. It was hard work and we were glad when at the end of summer the loft was finally full.

On the main floor a concrete slab between the two large adjacent doors helped with the removal of manure.

Over the years Dad saved the used oil from his tractor, car, and engine. The thick black oil, mixed with lampblack (purchased), was used to paint the roof. It was absorbed by the shingles, preventing them from drying out, and it also repelled rain and melting snow. Over the years, many hands applied paint to the barn. In the 1970s, we helped put a second coat of used oil on the roof.

I still ponder the design of the trusses. Did Dad design them himself or did he study a barn that he liked? Certainly there were no barns of that magnitude in the immediate neighbourhood.

The boards taken off the sides of the logs, called slabs, with rough bark on one side, were put to good use. They were used to construct tall fences around the yard and the pigpen. For many years our home resembled Fort Edmonton!

It would seem that the sawmill, whether bought or borrowed, was used primarily to prepare wood for the barn. After several years at the farm, it was gone.

I marvel at Dad's talent and skill as an architect and builder. He had a feel for design and construction. His barn withstood the test of time and has endured for more than half a century.

At one point during a recent visit I found myself alone in the barn. I studied the construction, ran my hand across the log wall, counted the trusses, and marvelled at my father's workmanship. I felt near to my dad, and it felt good.

Chapter 42 The River

The North Saskatchewan River is a powerful stream. Watercolour, 1985.

Flowing from the eastern slopes of the Rockies to Manitoba, the North Saskatchewan is one of the prairie's great rivers. It played an important role in the development of western Canada and because it rubbed shoulders with our homestead, it played an important role in our lives too.

The river, a short walk from our house, provided Sunday outings, a fishing spot, or a place for peaceful solitude. However, its might and merciless power also gave cause for concern. It brought sorrow as well as joy.

Recollections of my early visits to the river take me back to my pre-school years. As we made our way down steep slopes and through a wooded ravine, an older sibling held my hand and cautioned, "Hold on. Do be careful."

After the struggle through briar and bramble, the sudden view of the vast mass of water never failed to overwhelm me. Upon reaching the river we sat and relaxed, allowing the mesmerizing water to woo us into a peaceful state. I visualized York boats, laden with bales of furs and guided by strong men, glide swiftly downstream on their way from Fort Edmonton to Churchill. On the return trip, the boats would labour upstream with manufactured goods. Sometimes I visualized Pauline Johnson communicating with the elements, as I recited her poem "The Song My Paddle Sings."

She pleaded: "Be strong, oh paddle. Be brave, canoe. The reckless waves, we must plunge into."

During the spring the river ran high, making a walk along its banks hazardous and often impossible. However, in late summer when it ran low, the sound of the rapids could be heard at our home, less than a mile away. During those times, a walk along the bank was easy and we headed upstream, in search of a favourite cove, where uprooted trees, driftwood, debris, and occasionally articles from the big city of Edmonton washed ashore.

One day my brother Dan found a bottle with a note in it—an instant pen pal for the shy young man. Now and then a tennis ball bobbed up and down waiting to be claimed. A tennis ball was a precious find: first, because we could not afford such luxuries, and second, because our local shops did not carry them.

Not all our discoveries along the river were happy ones. One day we found a battered and decomposed body several feet above the bulk of the debris. The location of the corpse meant it had floated to our shores when the river ran high. The RCMP detachment in Two Hills was notified.

On a beautiful July morning, our neighbour Mary hurried towards our door. She and her husband John planned to pick saskatoons on the north side of the river. They would cross by boat and had room for one more person. It was bread-baking day so Mother could not go. She suggested that I was a fast picker and should join them.

With two large milk pails, some bread, cheese, and water, I joined our neighbours.

The boat, a crude, wooden, handmade effort, hinted at disaster.

Is it safe, I wondered? The boat had been anchored downstream, beyond a sharp bend in the river. Locals claimed that an eddy existed in the bend. Debris and logs disappeared at that spot and were spewed out several hundred feet downstream. As a result, it was important to avoid crossing through the eddy.

We glided easily with the current and John guided us safely to the opposite shore. The berries were plump and plentiful and we soon had six large heavy pails full of saskatoons. John feared that the extra weight would be too much for the frail boat. He would have to make two trips. Half the berries and Mary would go first.

John laboured to prevent the strong current from sweeping them downstream. The river was unrelenting, but they made it. When he returned for me, I was scared. As we left the shore, the boat sprang a leak. John reached behind him and hurled a can towards me.

"Bail. Bail fast!" he commanded. I was glad to be doing something.

"Thank you God," I whispered when we reached the south shore. The experience taught me to respect the power of the river even more than I had before.

The Desjarlais Ferry, two miles upstream, caused concern for horse-drawn wagons. The horses became frightened by the "clip-clop" of their own hooves on the ferry's wooden deck. I remember Father giving the reins to Mother. He would talk gently to the horses, guide them onto the ferry's platform, and then stand in front of the team during the crossing.

Over the years tragedies occurred on our river. One unlucky young girl was asked to deliver a letter to the ferryman. She accepted a ride across the river and back. A ferry malfunction threw her off the heavy plank she stood on. The ferryman instructed a passenger to guide the ferry to shore, while he jumped into the boat that accompanied the ferry. Although he tried to save her, he was able to retrieve only the body of the lifeless child.

In more recent years, a man struggled towards our farm gate. My brother John ran to meet him. There had been a helicopter accident on our shore. After phoning for an ambulance, we drove to within a short distance of the mishap.

We scrambled down the riverbank, to the scene of the accident. A dazed man sat on the shore, while a young woman lay near the water, with the waves lapping at her body. Every now and then she groaned in pain.

John, who knew and taught first aid, checked the man and talked to the lady.

"Can you help her?" I pleaded. But he shook his head. "We can't move her," he advised. We waited for the ambulance. His hunch was right. She had a broken back.

One of the saddest tragedies occurred one Sunday afternoon, when several young men in the community gathered at the river. They yelled and laughed as they tried to communicate with a group of young people on the opposite shore. Stephen, a close family friend, yelled to the other group over the swishing sound of the moving water. Should he swim across? His mind was soon made up. Too soon. Confident in his swimming skills, he did not listen to his friends. He jumped into the water. A few strong strokes took him into the main stream. His head was

The North Saskatchewan River, 1990.

seen above water until he reached the bend in the river. Then he disappeared. Did the cold water cramp his muscles? Did he land on shore beyond the bend or did he swim into the eddy? We could only speculate.

To make matters worse, Stephen was fond of my oldest sister, Gladys. She had to be told, and who would do it? Almost two months later his decomposed body was found in the province of Saskatchewan.

Probably my happiest recollection of the river occurred when I was in fourth grade. It was summer and the water was low. We visited our favourite cove. Among the dead branches and other debris was a tennis ball. It bobbed up and down with the movements of the water. I had found it. It was my ball.

My ball was in great demand on rainy days, when the official softball, requisitioned by the school board, could not be taken outdoors. With a tennis ball and bat, however, we could play a game called Rounders.

Two eighth grade captains chose sides. They did not pick children below fifth grade. The teams had been decided. I put my hands over my face and turned my back to the group. Immediately I felt a hand on my shoulder. It was my brother Steve.

"Why are you crying?" he asked.

"It's not fair," I sobbed. "It's my ball and they won't let me play." Within seconds, I too was chosen. In fact, I played ball on all wet days and developed my skills in catching, throwing, and batting—skills that stayed with me throughout my life.

The river was an important force in our lives: beautiful and serene, powerful and mighty, feared and respected.

Chapter 43 Good Intentions Gone Bad

The little house that Dad built. Hairy Hill, 1943.

"Will someone look after the chop?" Mother pleaded as she kneaded a big batch of dough. She looked up from her work. Silence. No responses. Nick lay dozing on the sofa. Kathleen was clearing the breakfast table and Steve had been flipping through the Eaton's catalogue. But hearing Mother's request, he quickly grabbed the slingshot that lay on his lap and pretended to be busy whittling.

"Nick, you do it today and you will save yourself a trip if you take the slops and skim milk down with you."

Nick reluctantly got up and sauntered towards the full buckets. His beanpole frame required him to bend down a long way to reach the handles. As he made his way outdoors he grumbled and complained about how he had to do so much work while others took it easy.

Mother needed much help that summer, as Dad spent most of his time constructing a house in Hairy Hill. The "little house" was built to allow the younger children to continue their education. She managed as best as she could, to avoid placing more stress on her husband. We children helped wherever possible, but not always willingly.

Doing the "chop" meant going downhill near the slough where the hungry pigs grunted and squealed at the sight of anyone approaching. Our dad believed that the pigs would be ready for market much sooner if they were fed cooked grain rather than dry food.

He set up the area by supporting a small metal drum on stones, at an angle, leaving enough room under it for a fire. A shallow well nearby supplied water. With the water table high because it was near a slough, it required only two or three pulls on the rope to draw water. When the water heated, it was ladled over two tanks half full of chopped grain. Stirring with a wooden paddle followed. It was important that all the grain be moistened. Then it would cool off during the day to be ready for the evening's feeding and the next morning's pig breakfast.

Summer holidays had come. Our parents would get help from us while there were more hands to help with the many farm chores. They would not have to do the chop any more. The extra help would look after that.

I had just turned thirteen and had completed the country school curriculum. Although I did not concern myself with my future plans, I felt somewhat grown up and felt I should become more responsible. A stage in my life had been completed.

I disliked doing dishes and housework. I preferred to work outdoors. So I decided to take over the chop duties.

Each morning I methodically made my way down the hill, remembering the skim milk and slops. First I filled the metal drum with water and lit the fire. I set the lid firmly over the opening so the water heated faster. In the meantime, I fed the previously prepared porridge and house leftovers to the pigs and then filled the two tanks half full with the chopped grain stored in the granary. While near the granary, I fed grain to the chickens, turkeys, and geese.

When the water heated, it was ladled over the chopped grain in the two tanks. It smelled almost good enough to eat. No wonder the pigs ate it with gusto. They slopped, put their forefeet into the trough, grunted, and slurped. The cats and dog followed later to lick the trough clean.

My chosen job went superbly during most of the summer. I felt happy and content. The family was happy too and there were no threats of firing me.

But one fateful day all that changed. I must have been extra conscientious that day. A roaring fire was built and the water heated quickly. When I pried off the lid, the pressure in the boiling water sent the lid flying, and water burst forth like a volcano. It happened too fast! It gushed over one side of my lower limbs, scalding much of my leg. I experienced excruciating pain! My chop days were over. The following days I lay on the sofa with my leg on a pillow. Nick did not like that.

By then the summer was almost over and I would soon be leaving the farm to live in the new house that Dad built, where I would continue with my schooling.

During my recovery, the old routine returned. Each morning Mother pleaded: "Will someone look after the chop?"

Chapter 44 Hairy Hill During the War Years

I can't remember the last time I was in Hairy Hill but I sometimes wonder about the town that was my first home away from home.

By 1940 I had completed grade eight—the top grade taught at the Deep Lake country school. At that time I don't recall being concerned about my future. After their country-school education was over, most young people helped their parents at the farm and later married and began their own lives on farms. The occasional courageous and daring young person took the train to Edmonton and sometimes found employment there. Cash in one's pocket was rare but desperately desired.

There was always much to do at the farm. I plunged into the routine of helping with chores and seasonal work.

At that time Steve stayed with a Toma family near Hairy Hill to help transport their children to school by sleigh in winter and buggy in spring. That gave him an opportunity to study beyond grade eight. After two years that family no longer needed him. That was when Father bought a lot for $200 in Hairy Hill and that summer sacrificed commitments at the farm to build a small house in town. The house had no electricity, no running water, and no phone. But in spite of that, the house made it possible for us to continue our studies.

That fall, at the age of thirteen, I left the security of farm and family to venture into the unknown. Our parents decided that our younger siblings George, Lucille, and Bertha (Beth), and later Adeline, would also live with us. Town schools where a teacher concentrated on one grade only would be superior to a country school where one teacher taught eight grades. Besides, they would not have to walk the long three miles to school each day, come rain or snow.

Hairy Hill was only twelve miles from the farm but in those days that was a considerable distance. By that time our dad was one of a very few farmers who owned a car. Snow ploughs and antifreeze were unheard of so the car sat idle during the winter months. With horses, the trip to town and back took a whole day. Most neighbours travelled to town with horses.

Five people were a lot of bodies for the small dwelling. Steve and George crawled into the attic space to sleep. They dressed sitting on the floor. Although cooking was never my favourite pastime, the family had to be fed. One change of

Pearl at CPR Hairy Hill Station, 1947.

clothing was worn all week long. During the fall and spring when travel by car was possible, we generally spent the weekends at the farm and got a clean set of clothes. Our food supply for the week also travelled back with us. However, the cellar in the little house had potatoes so there was no need to go hungry. Winter months were difficult because cold spells sometimes prevented a weekly trip to town for our parents. Those trips were by horse and cutter. During those periods we fended for ourselves without the luxury of even buying a loaf of bread.

Some teachers questioned our living alone without parents. Steve, at seventeen, could not be regarded as an adult. However, we "kept our noses clean" and no action was taken.

While a youngster, I heard neighbours talk about H-aa-rr-y Hill. Later I learned that the name was derived from a *hairy* hill where the buffalo slept and shed their old coats of hair.

I soon discovered that the main street ran down the slope from south to north. The street continued down a rough, curved trail through a grassy slope to the railway station at the bottom of the hill.

One of the buildings on the main street was the impressive Imperial Lumber Company. Its manager was a Mr. Samograd. While in twelfth grade, Steve was employed there after school and felt blessed to get the job and earn a few dollars. Just north of the grand building, a small convenience store run by Orest Arechk and his wife was an attraction for high school students. During lunch breaks the store's narrow aisle was crowded with students, but our family was forbidden to go there. In fact we were not allowed to go into any buildings. Our instructions were that we go to school and return home with no meandering. Because we had no money, there was no purpose in going into stores.

Across the street from the lumber store was a pool hall. Our parents forbade us to ever go into that place. I did not know what a pool hall was and was curious. The few times I went past it I glanced towards the window to see why it was an evil place and why it was out of bounds.

In the northeast corner of the same block stood a progressive general store run by Mr. George Michalcheon and his assistant, Mr. Hauca. A similar but smaller store in the next block owned by a poor business man did not do well. Times became difficult. Rumours had it that he set fire to his business in order to claim the insurance and feed his poor family. Sadly, he perished in the basement of the building.

At the bottom of the block stood a barbershop, the community hall, and the hotel. Across the main street from the hotel Mr. Olewich ran a machine shop. His son Thaddeus was in my grade.

A couple of small streets on the west side of Main bordered the school grounds. In the winter a boarded hockey rink provided entertainment for fans, including girls standing in the cold in their then-popular nylon stockings hoping to meet Mr. Right. Slacks were still a "no-no."

East of Main on a small street was the blacksmith shop run by a Mr. Kowalchuk. Near it a pump and water trough served the horses that drew farm wagons into town but also for homes in the area. Water was carried by pail. Down that slope north of the water pump stood the Zukewski house where the farm children stayed to attend high school. Another student house stood between the Zukewski house and ours.

The Straty family lived across the street from us. Mr. Straty owned a dray that transported mostly supplies from the train station to the businesses in town. The post office, manned by Mr. Lisigor, was south of the main street.

After nearly a decade of the Depression, money became more plentiful. It seems that the war helped make the difference and that period was the beginning of Hairy Hill's growth.

The community strove for progress. Women wanted stylish clothes even though they rarely had the money to buy them. They looked for something different, often visiting the Salvation Army stores in more progressive centres. Kerchiefs gave way to hats. Nylon stockings were the rage but were not readily available, and girls who wore them often checked the backs of their legs to make sure the seams were straight. High-heeled shoes were popular. Dress and skirt lengths rose. Young men wore their military uniforms with pride; in most cases the uniform was the first real suit of clothes they owned. They walked the streets with an air of superiority.

The train was the most practical mode of transportation. It travelled east from Edmonton to Lloydminster one day, returning the following day, transporting passengers as well as goods. On Thursdays, heavy cans full of cream covered an area on the station platform. Each can had the name of an Edmonton dairy and the shipper's name brightly painted on its sides. On the return trip, empty cans waited on the platform to be picked up. Livestock and poultry as well as grain brought to the elevators near the tracks were shipped by freight trains. Men in the services depended on the free travel by trains.

During the war years Hairy Hill's population and economy was on an upward swing. When I left Hairy Hill after high school, it was a growing town.

Part of my heart will always be with Hairy Hill. I am indebted to the town and school that helped guide the course of my life.

Chapter 45 Memories of the Second World War

John and RCAF buddies in England, 1943.

"Brush your teeth. One day you want to be a lady with nice teeth," instructed my oldest brother John.

Life was fine at the age of nine. Why would I want to be a lady? The future did not exist. I was content where I was.

Fifteen years my senior, he felt it his responsibility to set good examples for his siblings. At every opportunity John talked to us younger folk about good man-

John in the RCAF, 1944.

ners, about consideration for others, and about the importance of being truthful and honest. Nor did he tolerate poor posture.

"Stand tall. Shoulders back. Head high but chin in. Tummy in." He did not foresee the near future when he would be under similar command.

In the mid-1930s, John had joined the Alberta Dragoons, and in June of 1939 was a mounted escort at the King George VI and Queen Elizabeth visit to Edmonton. By September of that year, Canada was at war. Young men from

John and buddies overseas, 1943.

our farming community were being conscripted into the army. However, John disliked the army, so he volunteered to serve in the Royal Canadian Air Force. He was accepted, despite a meagre ninth grade education. Dan, a younger brother, followed John's example and also joined the RCAF.

The village of Hairy Hill now saw the occasional young man in uniform stride down one of its two streets. Young ladies' hearts "skipped a beat" when they saw a soldier home on furlough. Before the days of uniforms, the young men rarely got a second glance.

While John and Dan trained for war, I graduated from eighth grade at Deep Lake school. I was now attending high school in the town of Hairy Hill.

One morning, my parents and John arrived at our door. All appeared distraught. John had been visiting the farm during his last furlough in Canada.

"We'll take you to the station," I heard my father say.

"No. I'd like to go alone."

Tearful goodbyes followed. It was the only time I saw my father cry. The emotional sight was too much for me so I grabbed my books and slipped out the door. John quickly followed. With duffle bag slung over his shoulder, he called, "Study hard. Take care."

He forced a smile, then turned quickly and strode down the grassy slope towards the railway station. I took the uphill shortcut to the school. As I hurried, I visualized my parents clinging to each other in silent prayer. I imagined them gazing out the lone north window of the little house. They would hear the train's whistle, see it rumble to a stop, and watch their firstborn climb aboard.

The full impact of my brother's overseas posting slowly became clear. Blue, thin *air mail* letters arrived sporadically. Some had words blocked out. We could only guess at the complete contents of a sentence. Censored! But the whole family eagerly awaited more news. We wrote often to both John and Dan and sent parcels.

As the war escalated, Father spent every spare moment listening to the radio for war news. Neighbours who did not have radios, or who did not understand English, spent evenings in our home, absorbing Father's translation of the news.

There were rumours of deserters in the community. Some men home on leave did not return to their posts. Assisted by their families, they went into hiding. Neighbours noted sightings of the RCMP patrolling the district, and notified those in hiding. Many did not accept the purpose of a war that was fought across the Atlantic. It was not their war.

Other families prayed for their sons' safe return.

The years passed. Our parents continued to send letters and parcels overseas. I continued to care for my younger siblings while concentrating on my studies.

During the summer break at the farm, we picked berries, canned preserves, milked cows, gardened, and helped with haying. The list of tasks never ended.

At long last the war was over. Both John and Dan were safe. Dan's last post was in Vancouver, where he married and made that city his home. But we had little news from John. It seemed he would remain in England forever.

I was now in my senior year at Hairy Hill High. One of my extra-curricular activities was the school's sewing club. As a reward for our sewing efforts, five girls, including me, were chosen to spend two weeks in July at the Olds School of Agriculture, about two hundred miles away. Final exams and the scheduled trip were foremost in my mind. This would be my first trip away from home and family. I was both excited and nervous.

On arriving at the college I discovered, much to my delight, that I had a bedroom of my very own. I felt like a queen and savoured every moment spent in that room. After a rewarding and educational experience, I looked forward to reporting my adventures to my family.

On the return trip, I spent one night in the city of Edmonton, with friends of an older sister. After the girls left for work the next morning, I timidly explored the big city. I walked back and forth, over several blocks, to fully understand the street numbering system. That, I decided, would be a story to share with my family. After hours of exploring, I worried I might miss my train to Hairy Hill so I headed for the station.

I arrived at the CPR station on the northeast corner of Jasper Avenue and 109 Street in plenty of time. As I waited, I indulged in a favourite pastime: people-watching, I noticed two military men at the far end of the room. Men in uniform were rarely seen now that the war was over. Those men wore the familiar RCAF uniform. One stood tall with shoulders back and head held high. He reminded me of my brother John. I felt guilty. With the recent events in my life, my thoughts seldom dwelt on my brother.

I continued to stare at the men but could not see their faces, so I moved to another spot. Gosh! The taller one looked like John, I thought. He is John! I approached slowly. I could be wrong. The man had a fine moustache bordering his upper lip. He gave me a casual glance. Then he looked again. I smiled.

"Why, if it's not my little sister! What are you doing here? My, how you have grown!"

John said goodbye to his friend and we boarded the train. As we travelled east towards Lloydminster, he wanted to know all about the family, about the farm, and about my studies. But every now and then he looked at me with a twinkle in his eye and repeated, "My, how you have grown."

I wanted to ask him about the war but refrained. John did not offer to talk about it for a long time after his return. Eventually we learned that he was posted in England. He had a motorcycle he used to go to classes and get around. He flew over enemy territory several times—east as far as the Ploesti oil fields in Romania. He told us how, when the sirens sounded and bombs fell, people ran to air raid shelters or sometimes into the path of a falling bomb. He claimed that he never ran. He put his trust in God. He also told us how much the letters and parcels meant. He shared the parcels with his friends. The long ocean voyage across the Atlantic to Europe was exhausting but he was delighted to fly back in a military plane. Regular commercial flights across the Atlantic did not exist at that time. He apologized for not letting us know that he was on his way home.

When the train arrived at Hairy Hill, John followed me as we disembarked. Our brother Steve was there to meet me. But when he spotted John he choked with emotion. He could not speak. John, always in command, eased the awkward moment. He nodded towards me.

"My, how she has grown. She's a fine young lady."

Pearl and John after John returned from overseas, 1945.

Chapter 46 She Made a Difference

While on the topic of Hairy Hill, I'd like to share another memory. I give credit to a fine person in my life for making my first trip out of Hairy Hill possible—at the age of sixteen, by train, to the School of Agriculture in Olds. That was a memorable first for me. The trip was the result of the work accomplished in a sewing club organized by this fine lady.

At the age of thirteen, life in town without parents or friends was lonely and frightening. My younger siblings and I were living on our own in the small house that Dad had built for us.

Ninth grade passed as in a mirage and I cannot even remember the teachers' names. In tenth grade, Miss Dugay from the United States found her way to Hairy Hill, Alberta. Her short but sturdy-looking stature and smartly coiffed curly and greying hair presented a striking figure. She walked tall with shoulders back and head held high. Her posture suggested that she would do well in the armed forces. Miss Dugay was different.

Immigrants, mostly from Europe, comprised the town and surrounding community. They had experienced difficult times and concentrated on hard work to keep their families alive. There was little time for the finer things in life. With no available media during that period, they had not heard of popular figures like Emily Post. Many did not even speak English. Although they encouraged their children to be kind and helpful, their "P"'s and "Q"'s were lacking.

Looking back, I now know that Miss Dugay was appalled by the lack of manners in the school. Matters came to a head one morning as she approached the front door of the school. Two boys ran past her and let the door slam in her face. They did not even say, "Good morning!" That type of behaviour was not acceptable and she would certainly do something about it.

Although Miss Dugay taught English and French, being proud of her heritage, she felt compelled to spend the full period teaching her first language, French. She was a fine French teacher. However, the time spent in English would have to include other incidentals besides nouns and verbs and adjective clauses.

After the slam-in-the-face incident, she marched into our classroom and

Miss Dugay instilled an appreciation for art. Watercolour, 2003.

began the period teaching etiquette. Her opening remarks went something like this: "I am a lady and I expect to be treated as such. From now on, when I enter this room, I expect you young men to stand. You will sit only after I nod."

What? The whole student body was shocked. That had never happened before. What kind of teacher was this?

The next time Miss Dugay entered our room, the boys slowly shuffled out of their seats. Some stood smartly while others, red-faced and embarrassed, slouched and looked at the floor or leaned on their desks. That would never do! Miss Dugay would have them "ship-shape" if it killed her. It did not take long before the boys stood at attention and looked smart.

Did Miss Dugay miss her calling? There was a war going on. She would have made a fine commander-in-chief in the Canadian army.

As the years rolled on, when necessary, part of the English period was devoted to activities other than English. Miss Dugay succeeded in polishing Hairy Hill High into young people whose manners were admirable. Boys opened doors for female students. Girls acknowledged the polite gestures. Boys offered to carry girls' books. "Please" and "thank you" replaced "gimme" and "ugh." Respect oozed from every pore.

The homesteaders' children were being prepared for the outside world. They could enter it with confidence because they now knew how people were expected to behave.

Miss Dugay's efforts continued throughout the many years she taught at the school. But not all students appreciated her efforts. Some mimicked her behind her back. They silently followed her with noses in the air. Some thought the time taken from English was wrong, but as by osmosis, they too absorbed the new information. Of course, they would never admit it.

Over the years my younger brother and sister also experienced the "Dugay doctrine." One day Miss Dugay met our mother on the street. During their friendly chat she remarked, "When your children are at the farm they are all yours, but when they are in town, I like to have them under my wing." The remark was a comfort to our mother and she remembered it.

Following our departure from Hairy Hill High, when Miss Dugay met one of our family members, she always inquired about those of us who found comfort "under her wing." Not only was she a fine teacher, but also a good friend who helped and cared. She made a difference.

Later, Miss Dugay became Mrs. Ruptash, when she married a local widowed farmer. They both enjoyed dancing and retired in Two Hills.

Chapter 47 A Close Call

Muddy roads in the spring. Pastel, 1985.

During the month of April patches of snow lingered in low and shady spots. Snow remained in ditches along the country roadsides and in dips in the road. But in time, summer would come again and the mud holes would become dry.

Father looked forward to the day when he could make the first spring trip to Hairy Hill by car. It would be comfortable, save precious time, and relieve the horses of a long, tiring trip. The 1927 Essex would stir again after resting all winter in storage.

Even though the dirt roads were barely dry, Father decided to get the car ready. He reinstalled the batteries that had been stored indoors all winter. He

Sandra was distressed on the trip to the hospital. 1947.

changed the oil, cleaned the spark plugs and carburetor. He checked the timing and the tires and filled the gasoline tank. Because there were still nights when the mercury fell below freezing, he would not put water into the radiator yet.

Father was well acquainted with the twelve miles of road to Hairy Hill. He knew every low spot that sometimes gave him trouble. One such spot was only a mile from home. He used it to gauge the condition of the roads. He estimated that after one more week of warm and sunny weather he might venture forth by car. In the meantime he would concentrate on getting his implements ready for the spring planting.

While Father worked near his workshop, he noticed Elena, a neighbour, standing in front of the summerhouse. She was talking with Mother. Her arm gestures suggested a serious subject. As he glanced towards the women, Father wondered, was something going on? It gave him an eerie feeling: a feeling that somehow he would be involved. And he did not like it. Then as Elena hurried off towards the gate, Mother headed towards him. The haste in her step bothered him.

"Sandra is in labour and is having a hard time," Mother gently but urgently began. "She must get to a doctor right away."

Generally homesteaders' wives delivered their babies at home with a neighbour as midwife. Cases were rare where women needed a doctor.

Sandra was expecting her first child. She lived over the hill with her husband and Elena, her mother-in-law. The plan was that the mother-in-law would assist with the birth when the time came. But the young woman was experiencing difficulties.

"Why are you telling me this?" Father asked, knowing full well what was implied. He bent over and took an unusually swift swing with the hammer at a disc plate. Then, before Mother could say anything more, he added, "The roads are too muddy for travel by car. I will have nothing to do with this."

In a soft but urgent voice, Mother continued. "You must try, Fred. The lives of two people depend on you."

"Why me?" he questioned. "I'm staying out of this." The responsibility was more than he wished to handle. He could not be sure that he could get to the Willingdon Hospital safely or in time. He rarely travelled to that town and did not know the condition of those roads. He was annoyed with his wife for mentioning the problem at all. Why should he be put in such a position? But his car was the only one in the area.

Driving under unpredictable road conditions was stressful and hazardous at most times. But being responsible for a woman in labour made it so much worse. Often quick choices had to be made when a driver approached a mud hole. Should he speed up and fly across? Should he shift into a low gear and move through slowly? Or should he stop and study the situation first? Sometimes the car was inched back and forth until it pointed back home.

Father did not like the predicament he was in at all. He wondered why the birth was not quick and quiet like those his wife experienced. That was the way babies should be born. Why did they need to go to a hospital?

While he thought of excuses to avoid the responsibility, he felt a tug on his arm and a gentle voice urging, "You must try to help this poor woman. She has been in labour for hours. Please help her. Please."

"I need water for the radiator. Get me some water."

With one hand supporting her back and the other holding on to Elena, Sandra waddled to Father's car and reclined on the back seat. Elena handed her a pillow and a towel and then sat in front.

Father approached his first hurdle a mile from home. He studied it quickly, then shifted into a lower gear. Slowly but with enough power, he dropped into the mire. The wheels spun and spun, but inch after inch he slowly moved forward out of the hole and onto solid ground.

He thought of the patient in the back seat and wondered which was more important. Should he drive fast to save time even though the roads were bumpy, or should he consider the comfort of his ward by slowing down at every bump?

Now and then a muffled groan was heard from the back seat. He knew that time was an important factor. He preferred that the birth not occur in his car, and not while he was hopelessly stuck in the mud.

The road west towards Willingdon had several low spots but presented no real problems. He rejoiced when he saw the town ahead. He also realized that the panting and groaning from the back seat had become more intense and constant.

"Look. There's Willingdon," he called, hoping that his charge would feel better. He breathed a sigh of relief as he approached a small rise in the road. In a few minutes they would be there. However, when he reached the crest of the hill, his heart sank. Before him lay a large body of water. Water covered the road and extended well into the fields on both sides.

"Oh, no," he groaned. "What do we do now?"

The noises from the back seat obstructed his thinking. The young woman sounded as though she was in utter distress. Elena tried to comfort her. She had just told Sandra that Willingdon was in sight.

Father knew that he could not travel farther. He got out of the car, removed his hat, and wiped his sweaty brow. "Oh Lord," he whispered, as he scanned the horizon as if for answers. Then, with an instant glimmer of hope, he quickly opened the back door and looked down at a young woman whose face showed fear and pain. Wisps of hair clung to her wet face.

"Come," he called gently. He helped Sandra out of the car. "Put your arms around my neck and hold on tight." As the bulging woman held on, he remembered his wife's words, "the lives of two people depend on you." The two lives were now in his hands.

He felt the cold, knee-deep water fill his leather boots.

"What do you think you're doing?" Elena called angrily. Father ignored her and pushed onward. When he reached dry ground, he lowered Sandra, set her on his jacket and then ran up the road.

"Why is he leaving us?" It was Elena again.

Up the road, Father had spotted a farmhouse with a car parked near it. Moments later the car and the new driver pulled up. They helped Sandra into the waiting car as Elena walked out of the frigid water in bare feet, with a shoe in each of her outstretched hands. Father watched as they headed towards the hospital and then quickly turned and waded back across the water to his car. He sat behind the wheel and rested his head on it. Then he took several deep breaths.

"Whew! That was close! Too close." His big hands shook as he inched his car back and forth until it pointed homeward.

"It was close call," he answered Mother as he drained the water from the radiator and then strode towards the shop.

"What happened?" Mother repeated anxiously as she tried to keep up with his long stride.

"It was too close," he repeated. "And don't put me in a spot like that again!"

She was well aware that her husband was upset. As a rule, he met challenges head on but this one was different. Even though she felt partly responsible for the anxiety it caused him, she was comforted that his efforts were not in vain.

Chapter 48 Schools and Education

Pearl with pupils at Deep Lake, 1949.

Father's four years of schooling in his homeland served him well. I remember him doing sums in his head faster than I could do them on paper. All his life, he was well aware of the importance of learning. But what opportunities for learning were in the cards for his family? He had to wait and see. As his family grew, it was his nature to take the little opportunities that crossed his path to cultivate interest and curiosity. Mother, on the other hand, taught her family to be kind, helpful, and humble. Calmly, she put a damper on stressful situations. The family depended on her for emotional strength.

John and Gladys, the two oldest children in our family, did not begin school at age six. Why? It was simple. There were no schools in the community. The first school they attended briefly was the newly completed Ispas School, three and one half miles away. I believe that they started school together. I remember Gladys recalling that she sometimes helped her older brother with math problems. She was pleased with herself.

When the Deep Lake School was completed, they transferred to that school. It was only three miles away, a half-mile closer than Ispas. Our homestead was on the west side of the dividing road that ran north and south; all settlers on the west side belonged to the Deep Lake district while those on the east belonged to Ispas.

During those early days most teachers were male and had English backgrounds. Mr. Thompson was the first teacher at Deep Lake. Several years later Mr. Manson took over. By that time Mike had joined his older siblings and a couple of years later Dan and then Helen followed.

The early teachers occasionally visited Dad and Mother because they were some of the few adults in the district who spoke some English. (Mother learned it while living with the Edmunds after her mother Sanfira died and Dad seemed to pick up English while working on the railroad, in the mines, and on the High Level Bridge in Edmonton, before he applied for a homestead.)

Mother would invite the teachers to share a simple meal and, as she had done all her life, shared farm produce including bread, eggs, cheese, butter, milk, and potatoes. The teacher "batched" in a teacherage situated west of the school.

During my growing-up years, I had a feeling that Dad was regarded as the black Romanian sheep in an otherwise Ukrainian fold. Several incidents that occurred with neighbours hinted at that feeling. There were two other Romanian families. The Yurkos, who lived farther south, had one son who was considerably older than our family. I doubt that he completed eight years of schooling. The Hrenuiks, west of us, had very poor land and eventually left the district.

Our dad often cautioned us about our association with the other children. We were to *keep our noses clean*. One day, when in about fifth grade, I broke Father's rule. During those days when there were no telephones, messages or gossip were sent in letters through the children. A girl who walked in our direction asked me to accompany her to deliver a letter to a family on the Ispas side of the road. That was one-quarter of a mile off our beaten path. She promised that we would run there, deliver the letter, and then catch up with our siblings in the remaining mile home.

When we got there, Mrs. Bujak gave us each a cookie. The two spoke in their language while I feared that I was going to be in trouble. I nudged the girl but she didn't budge. At last we left and ran the whole mile home. Apparently my siblings, knowing I was going to be in trouble, walked very slowly. They even stopped and waited. But we just took too long so they went home. Dad immediately noticed that I was missing. Minutes later, when I arrived, Dad marched up one side of me and down the other! I wished that he would whip me and get it over with. He did not hurt me but just reminded me over and over that I was expected to go straight to school and then back home. He would not tolerate my wandering all over the community. Being humiliated and used as an example in front of the rest of the family made me wish that I could sink through the floor.

There seemed to exist a certain amount of jealousy towards our family. That was probably so because our family did well at school, or because Mr. Thompson and later Mr. Manson visited our home, or because Dad, although a homesteader like the rest of the neighbours, was progressive and innovative. His truck and thresher were the first in the area. He understood machines. However, in time, our family became respected and accepted by the community. Some even married into our family.

By the time Helen, the fifth oldest in our family, began school, changes were occurring. The former teacher had been replaced by a female: Miss Ewanchuk. The local school board's secretary (school divisions did not exist) had the power to hire and fire teachers. He did not like Dad. Jobs were difficult to find and teachers feared firing.

It was during that period that Dad experienced some altercations with the school system. He theorized later that it likely began because the teacher, knowing that the secretary did not like Dad, would try to win favour by picking on Dad's children. Since we were good students she could not punish us for our schoolwork. But she picked on us in other ways. Dad ignored the negative reports we brought home, but he suspected that all was not right. The teacher's ultimate error happened when, with a yardstick, she whacked Helen, a timid and shy child in third grade, across the arm for some simple reason like dropping a pencil on the floor. When Helen returned home that day with a red welt across her little arm, Father took drastic action. He kept his children at home. The summerhouse became a temporary schoolroom and John, the oldest, taught his younger siblings the three R's. That action, of course, was contrary to the education laws. Eventually the children were returned to school. However, Dad had made a statement that affected all those involved and surprised the rest of the community. Now when I look back, I admire Dad's insight and courage.

As the older family members were finishing the last year of their formal education, grade eight, Nick and then Steve joined the school group. For several years there was an average of at least four of our family members attending school.

Our dad knew the value of education and hoped his family could continue beyond grade eight. But with no high school near, there was little he could do.

Although Dad was grateful for the opportunity to own his own land, and was up to the challenge of farming, he did not receive a regular paycheque. Farming was a gamble. Success depended mostly on the weather. For instance, the drought during the thirties could not sustain a family. Yet he could not foresee anything but farming for his children's future.

Arrangements were made for John to live with his aunt and uncle's family, the Harrisyms, in order for him to attend Moose Lake School where he could take his ninth and tenth grades. In addition to a small stipend for room and board, John was expected to do chores after school and weekends. But the arrangement was short-lived. John worked diligently after school: helped with the harvest, milked cows, and did chores. As the end of the first term approached and there were fewer chores during the winter, his aunt preferred not to have him live with them any more. Dejected, John returned home, and started walking to Shalka School (also called Little Boian) where ninth grade was taught—five and a half miles south of the farm. That was just too far to walk so he studied at home. I believe that in the spring he wrote the ninth grade departmental exams. Further studies for John were interrupted for about ten years, until after he returned from the war.

Opportunity? None. It saddens me when I think of the older half of our family whose lives might have been more fulfilling had they had the opportunity for further study. Yet learning does not end with the completion of a certain grade. Learning continues throughout one's lifetime: through conversations with others, through personal experience, and through the media. The basic studies completed in a country school served each of our family members well. But more would have been better.

As time went on, the pendulum began a slow swing to the right. Opportunities for further education were becoming more available but not without struggles.

I started school at Deep Lake at age six with Katie, who was seven. Nick and Steve went with us. Our teacher was Mr. Dzegolik. Part-way through first grade he advanced me to second grade. Four years later Mr. Braco and then Mr. Cucheran were our teachers.

When Steve finished Grade 8, the younger set moved to the "little house" in Hairy Hill. As a result, Steve, Lucy, Bertha, George, Adeline, and I completed high school.

Our parents decided that Kathleen, who was in eighth grade, would continue at Deep Lake and help at home with chores. By that time both Gladys and Helen were married. Mike died at age nineteen, and both John and Dan were with the RCAF. Katie's help was most important to our parents.

Except for Adeline and Bertha, who would eventually join the Hairy Hill gang, the farmhouse became quite empty.

The adjustment from the farm to town was hard on all of us. At age thirteen, I cooked, cleaned, got the young ones ready for school, and tried to study. At that time important departmental exams were given to ninth and twelfth grade students.

Although I was at the top of my class at Deep Lake, I was now competing with students who had had the benefit of a far better education than I had at a country school. I did not know how to study. At Deep Lake I always did my work at school and never had homework. It was a difficult year for us all being away from our parents, but with so many responsibilities it was especially trying for me. But by the grace of God I passed into tenth grade.

Our parents brought us clean clothes and supplies of food each week. We had no money to buy anything and our parents forbade us to go to stores. Once, during a cold spell, they did not make their usual Thursday market day trip. By the weekend we were out of bread. We could not buy any so I decided to try my hand at baking bread. I mixed a batter and set it to rise. Then, surprisingly, our parents arrived. Mother looked at my sad effort, added more water and flour, kneaded it well, and we had a good supply of bread that week.

The four of us who lived in the house were young; there were no adults. Our parents feared being reported. Now and then teachers asked Lucille and George if one of our parents was with us.

While Steve took his eleventh grade, Mr. Samograd, who managed the Imperial Hardware Store in town, asked Steve to assist him after school. Of course Steve was delighted and so were our parents. Steve was earning money! He saved enough to purchase a lot adjacent to the one where we lived. He began to build a house on his lot as the little house became crowded. Bertha joined our group and Adeline would soon follow.

Several years later Mr. Samograd retired. Steve eventually bought the store and learned much about business, people, and life as he ran his store and other businesses, and became an active member of the town council and a trustee in a school division. Learning continued for Steve.

The war effort reduced the availability of farm labour. In the fall the high school was closed for a week or two to allow the students to help with the harvest. In tenth grade my parents needed my help for an extra week. It was during that week that the basics in algebra were taught. I missed it. It was unfortunate because mathematics was always my strong subject. With God's help I got to twelfth grade.

I was the first in the Bidulock family to break the ice by attending university, and it warms my heart to think that my struggles may have influenced my siblings, and their children and grandchildren.

When George finished high school, he was well informed about further studies. His marks, especially in the sciences, were excellent. His interests leaned towards engineering. Because I had become a wage earner as a teacher, at $82 per month, our parents persuaded George to follow in my footsteps. They had confidence that he would do well as a teacher. Finally, George caved in and registered in Education. But he was not happy. When he arrived at the university in the fall, he immediately, and without parental consent, transferred to Engineering.

The cost of living in Edmonton and tuition were always a concern. The three residences on campus, Pembina, Assiniboia, and Athabasca, had limited space and were expensive.

Because George did not wish to be a financial burden to his parents, he joined an RCAF program, Royal Officer Training, which would help him through school provided he attended regular meetings and agreed to work three years with the RCAF after graduation. He accepted that.

By the time he graduated, George had married Rosa and with Jenise just a baby, he served the three years at Clinton, Ontario. On their return to Alberta they stayed at the farm for a spell and then George began studies towards an M.Sc. degree in Electrical Engineering. While Rosa was the breadwinner, George took courses, did his dissertation, and also cared for Jenise and baby Brian. Then he joined Alberta Government Telephones and had a successful career for many years. His hobbies—stamp collecting, polishing rocks, interest in special wood such as diamond willow and driftwood, bird watching, and gardening—were all learning experiences. He had a gift for remembering and telling jokes.

After beginning school at Hairy Hill in grade two, Lucille was successful in attaining her high school there and then studied education at the University of Alberta. She completed four years of university for a B.Ed. degree. She married and taught in Edmonton and Halifax. After the family's return to Alberta she took further courses towards a graduate certificate for a teaching librarian. She continued in her new career until her retirement. As a teaching librarian, she learned much.

Beth completed grades one to twelve at Hairy Hill. After completing her high school, she registered in the B.Sc. nursing program of four years. She lived in Nurses' Residence across the street, west of the University of Alberta Hospital. All nursing students in the program were required to live there. They had rules and regulations that were strictly administered. For instance, they had to be in residence by a certain time in the evenings. They were not to marry while in the program.

I remember my little sister in a cute pink frock with white starched apron, white stockings, and white shoes, as well as a cute white nurse's cap on her naturally curly hair. She looked professional when wearing this uniform and was easily distinguished as a member of the hospital staff.

Beth's learning continued in her work, especially in the many years of cancer research that she undertook at the University of Hawaii.

Adeline was not exposed to a country school experience except for two years when our parents insisted that she live with me in a teacherage at Brierfield school north of Derwent. Other than that she studied at Hairy Hill. She registered in Chemistry at U of A and earned her degree in four years. Her studies have provided her with a wealth of experiences, including government appointments and contributions of scientific papers for textbooks. She was also interested in travel, hiking, and music.

While the younger ones of the family were busy doing high school and university, John, who returned from overseas after the war, finally was able to resume his studies. With government assistance for returned men, he studied at Canadian Union College and received the equivalent of a B.A. degree.

During that time, I, who had only an interim war emergency teaching certificate after one year at university, took summer school courses towards a degree in education. But it was a slow process because I could take a maximum of two courses per summer. If it was a lab course, I could only take one. Some fifteen years later, after marrying and raising a family, I returned to university. I scheduled my courses so I could be at home when the children came home from school for lunch and after school. Finally, three years later, in 1970, I got my B.Ed. degree.

But my learning did not stop there. As time went on, I registered in adult and special interest courses: painting; writing; languages including French, German, Portuguese, and a refresher in Romanian; papermaking; wheat weaving; and winemaking. Working with the Hansard group at the Legislature and as a historical interpreter at Fort Edmonton added to my education. I am sure that everyone gains knowledge through workplace experiences. Learning is a lifelong process.

Chapter 49 From Homestead to University

Lucille (B.ED. 1957, M. of Library Science 1980), Bertha (B.SC. in Nursing 1959), and Pearl (B.ED. 1971).

Some call it luck; others coincidence. Some say it's being at the right place at the right time. But I call it the grace of God.

I was in my last year of high school when the principal had a talk with students in my grade. He told us that due to the war, a shortage of teachers existed. The country schools were particularly hard hit. Only a short stint at university would be required before one could go out to teach. I filled out a form, without fully understanding what it was all about. I was timid and had no close friend with whom to discuss things I did not understand. I didn't really know what a university was, and I didn't realize that I had just applied to attend one.

During the summer, as I helped at the farm, I received a letter—probably my very first letter ever. It was a response to the form I had filled out, and it said something about attending the University of Alberta and the dates I should be there. I did not know I had a choice.

The following weeks were frightening and stressful. I would be the first of four younger siblings to take the plunge. I had no benefactor as Pip did in Charles Dickens' *Great Expectations*. The whole experience was most stressful and intimidating. I was so naïve! Now when I look back I find it rather comical, but also sad. As well, I was not aware of the concern my parents experienced. The unknown loomed before me.

So was it luck, coincidence, and being at the right place at the right time that helped me, a homesteader's daughter, do the almost impossible? I look back on the many unusual experiences and choices I made and I thank God for the opportunity to attend university.

Chapter 50 Religion and Our Family

Malin Romanian Greek Orthodox Church of Holy Cross (after restoration), 1985.

When I look back on how our parents handled religion in the family, I marvel at their attitude. As we became adults, we had the freedom to worship in churches of our choosing. All the churches we chose were of the Christian faith. That was a comfort, I am quite certain, but of course, those were different times.

My parents came to Canada as children so it is unlikely that they remembered religious experiences or observations of their parents and grandparents. My recollection is that Dad's sisters and their families leaned towards the evangelical faith. I recall being in a church in Lac La Biche, and admiring Uncle John's craftsmanship. He had built the altar in that church. He worked with wood, like his father, my grandfather, Stefan.

Sunday School Group: Pearl and Kathleen with missionaries, 1950.

Probably because we lived in a predominantly Ukrainian Greek Orthodox community, my parents sometimes attended the church at Ispas. That was likely for convenience and acceptance. As a child I attended that church only a very few times. To me the church service and the building were mostly a curiosity—the huge candles, the tiny angels painted on a blue ceiling, the aroma of incense, the chanting, the robed priest who spoke in a language that I did not understand. It was all fascinating and interesting, but I did not learn much about God or the Bible. I do believe that most of my siblings experienced similar observations. We youngsters flowed with the tide. We did what our parents asked us to do.

Probably what influenced our lives and knowledge of the Bible most was the community visits by missionaries from the Prairie Bible Institute (PBI) at Three Hills. The ground-breakers were two young women who grew up north of the river. I was in elementary grades when they held Sunday School at our Deep Lake School as well as in homes that were open to them. Several years later Reverend Waldy and his family moved into the district. They rented a house across the road from the former Shalka Post Office. They, too, held meetings in schools and people's homes. Our parents opened our home to them. There, Mrs. Waldy accompanied the singing by playing the organ we had in our home. On warm summer Sundays, the music and singing of hymns floated through the barnyard. Some

Sunday School Group: Rev. Waldy and missionary plus families Bidulock, Hutzkal, Semenuik, Dubitz, and Huculak, 1950.

neighbours came to our house for the services; other Greek Orthodox believers had nothing to do with it.

In the summer two young women from PBI held Bible School, first in the small, abandoned Skoreko house and later in what was called the "Bull Corral," which was an open platform with limited shelter where dances were sometimes held during the summer. Since the moonshine ran freely at the dances, our parents discouraged us from attending. I had never been to one of those dances, but I spent summer days there helping the two missionaries with children's Bible School.

I think it was during that time that I learned Bible verses that have been a comfort to me throughout my life: "Jesus said, 'I am the Way, the Truth and the Life. No man cometh unto the Father but by Me'"; when tempted, "Get behind me Satan. I will follow the Lord and Him only will I serve."

Two favourites from Isaiah I often think of as I look over the fields. "I will lift up mine eyes unto the hills from whence cometh my help. My help comes from the Lord." When things go wrong, I remind myself, "This is the day which the Lord hath made. We shall rejoice and be glad in it."

During this time in history it is most important that God is part of our daily lives; honour Him before men and He will honour you in the kingdom of heaven.

When I was young I thought I would live forever. But life flashes by so quickly. However, it is a comfort to look forward to the *everlasting life* which He has promised as long as we accept Him as our Lord and Saviour. God keep and bless all our wonderful family, and families everywhere.

Epilogue

The baker's dozen became an even dozen after Mike's illness and early death, at nineteen years of age. As the older children became adults, they slowly left the nest but often returned to visit and help.

Eventually, the house became empty. Although Mother and Dad were alone, family members popped in every now and then. Perhaps due to their early commitment to the farm, they automatically pitched in to help—with cooking, house-cleaning, and gardening, but especially at harvest time.

My parents enjoyed relatively healthy lives. All their babies were born at the farm. Except for Mother's final few days, neither of them spent time in a hospital and neither took medication. Father died a few months before he reached his eightieth birthday and Mother was eighty-four when she died several years later.

Despite the struggles and challenges in owning their land and raising a large family, my parents were content with their lives. Their children were a comfort to them and their thirty-six grandchildren brought joy and many smiles.

The tree by the water. Watercolour, 2003.

The Tree by the Water

The tree near the water
Tall and strong
Lifts open arms
In rain and in sun

It stood for years
Among willow and fern
Lords over the valley
Roots hold it firm

Backrest for a hiker
Shade for a herd
Nesting for song birds
Cool spot for ferns

God's hand planted it
Where He wished it to be
May it dwell there ever
Throughout eternity

Marquis Book Printing Inc.

Québec, Canada
2010